WINDOWER

Windower

FIRST EDITION

Printed in the United States of America
ISBN 979-8-9897084-2-0

COVERT ARTWORK
Ocean Sea Cave by John Keith

DESIGN ≈ SEVY PEREZ
Text in Brandon Grotesque & Adobe Caslon Pro

This book is published by the
Cleveland State University Poetry Center
csupoetrycenter.com
2121 Euclid Avenue, Cleveland, Ohio 44115-2214

A CATALOG RECORD FOR THIS TITLE IS
AVAILABLE FROM THE LIBRARY OF CONGRESS

WINDOWER

MICHAEL LOUGHRAN

for MJ

“In the night, the Bad Lands became Good Lands.
I can’t explain it. That’s how it was.”

—John Steinbeck, *Travels with Charley*

“Let him brag in hell about that.”

—Aeschylus, *Agamemnon*

PS

On May 31st of the year in question, I came home to find my wife had died. I wrote this book to discover what my grief had been, or is.

In November of that same year, I fell in love again. I wrote this book, also, to learn how that could be.

I wanted to write a book about listening to Pharoah Sanders in grief. It was supposed to be called *PS*. "The book is not, at present, about jazz," MJ said after reading a few chapters.

I remember being at the beach the summer Noelle died and asking my father to listen to *Karma* with me. I laid my phone face-up on the kitchen table and we sat for the entire half hour of "The Creator Has a Master Plan," two heathens spending a week by the sea while grief jellied our insides. The racket of ecstasy sounded thin through my phone but I liked it that way. I never played it through headphones or speakers.

I liked it best with the phone in my back left pocket, its speaker facing up, a din that could move by walking but that would not leave me.

I don't think the music was teaching me anything. And as much as I played it, probably thousands of times drifting through days without contour and on loop while I slept, I don't think it healed me. I don't know for sure, but I guess I just loved it, and I think love is resistant to thought.

I don't remember if my father said anything when the song ended, or if he put his hand on my hand or on my back or if he called me "Mick," which is what he calls me.

OHIO

"Lots of the houses here have ponds," someone says to me, gesturing to a pond. The landscape is a mixture of agriculture and agricultural kitsch: a manicured yard with a large, decorative windmill looking out onto an actual cornfield. Actual birds, is my guess. But for all I know, the decorative windmill powers the whole town. So much turns out that way.

I'm new here. And worse than being new, I'm a widower—a widower courting a granddaughter. I've come all the way to Ohio, birthplace of David Allen Coe, to meet MJ's grandparents. The best David Allen Coe lyric is when he sings, "I sound a lot like David Allen Coe." Anything true is good to say. Air in the trees, air in the air. Widower by the pond, sharpening.

I'm worried my style of courtship will ring false, and worse, I'm worried the fear of falseness will inspire an overcorrection and I'll appear not only unsuited but also crazy. I'm also worried I'll curse, so in my head I repeat the word "fork" as a palliative treatment. "Who is this widower by the pond," I imagine the grandparents, with their many years of shared mind, thinking in unison, "with the sad eyes, mouthing the word 'fork' and overeating chips?" The grandfather asks me to spell my last name, which he writes down with care. He asks what it is I do for work.

*

I used to assign all kinds of things, but after Noelle died, I swept everything from the syllabus and assigned four different translations of the *Oresteia* by Aeschylus.

On the first day, I wrote the suffix of the tragedy, *-eia*, in huge letters on the board. "It means 'the bit about' or 'the little story of,'" I said, "so this is the little story of Orestes, our main character, whose father is murdered by his mother in the first play, who returns from exile to murder his mother in the second, and who in the third is hounded nearly to death by demon-monsters hellbent on murdering oath-breakers."

"Will they really read all four translations," my friends asked, and when I was in the mood for truth I told them it didn't matter, the point of a class is like the point of a book, which is to sneak something unpalatable into the minds of the willing. I only wanted to gain their trust, which would take time, and then ask them a question: *are the demon-monsters real?*

The weeks passed. Together, we pretended to read two of the translations. "Have the demon-monsters ever been real for you?" I asked one day, and scanned the room for knowing eyes. "Because I believe they have been real for me," I said. I timed this confession so it would land in the final moment before spring break, and then I went to meet MJ's grandparents.

*

In Ohio, one bird is aggrieved by others in the cattails. What is fear is really shame, is what it is. I have done all this before, is what the shame is. No one can help me remember the Lorrie Moore story about this conundrum, in which one divorcee fucks another in the style of fucking to which she became accustomed during her long marriage. Another

Lorrie Moore story I would like to remember is the one where a tree grows through the floor inside an old house, which is a metaphor for not worrying too much.

I look into the cattails, eating chips in the style to which I've become accustomed, and wonder about the birds. "How simple it could be in a story," I thought, "to become a windower instead." The story wants to be original but if it works, it won't have been. It fails, so it succeeds.

*

Two days into our visit, MJ's grandfather dies suddenly. We bury him in the cemetery near the house, by the hot as gold cornfield. The priest's book seems too large for a Bible and he never puts it down. "What am I thinking of," is how he begins many of his sentences—a bad memory or a rhetorical technique, it's hard to say: "What am I thinking of . . . Oh! The Gospel of John, it's different from the others, as you know." His vestments look expensive from a distance but cheap up close. His whole body is squinting. It's Tuesday. The homily on grief is settling into each of us, a balm he's been mixing for years. If you could stay here in the tent with the priest's sentences forever, you would be okay, but you can't do that, the gravediggers are waiting. Afterwards, like always, is where everything must take place.

Inside the burial tent, the priest is making a taxonomy of grief: "What am I thinking of?" he asks. "Oh! There are better and worse ways to grieve, as we see when Jesus dies." The holiness of grief, the numinous concussion it bestows, its righteousness, this is the subject of the priest's homily. Like everything, it begins in biology but eventually takes a rhetorical form. Taije wrote a poem about the time she saw me cry in my sleep the summer Noelle died; Dave heard her read it and called me from the reading, his heart on a stick, his night ruined. Don't forget: it was the weepers Plato really wanted to banish.

"Am I going to get saved from this he asked and I said no," goes Taije's poem. "His eyes were wrong," it goes. I remember the day of her poem. We got bored of the museum and went outside to roll a joint in the wind. If I say "like penguins," you'll understand. It was a bad joint but it was ours. We needed more advice than was available. I didn't know MJ's grandmother yet, to whom I'll recommend walking up and down her driveway in the first days after her grief blooms: "You are always someone else," says the poem, says the priest, says Plato, and we were walking slowly, we didn't realize it at the time but we were walking, stoned, to her car. The day was already over. The sun was only a sneeze.

*

The demon-monsters are called Furies. Here is what they do: they seek those of us who have broken an oath. They find us and punish us to death. Here is how they do it: by hounding us creatively. Here is what they are: chthonic deities, meaning they come from underground, from deep inside the earth where the darkness has a smell. Here is what they have for hair: snakes. Here is what they have for heads: dog heads with bloodshot eyes. Here is how we die when they find us: in torment.

After spring break, I asked it directly: "Has anyone ever seen a Fury?" One student, dressed in black—his name was

Yogev—allowed his eyes to meet mine. It was tentative, this moment when we finally gave the slip to the smokescreen and met soul to soul, me and Yogev, the only student who had ever seen one. *Good good good*, I thought.

*

I hadn't packed for a funeral, so the tie I wear to the cornfield is the grandfather's, and the socks. I cry more than I expect. He was kind and careful and brilliant. The time he bought a small boat, sank it, got another. That he never cursed but liked those who did. At each of these I cry.

After the funeral, the grandmother looks through me with the wrong eyes and says, "This happened to you, too?" She says, "When he was laying there, when he was gone, I wanted to lay down with him."

The day after the grandfather dies, we buy the very fast car. We have no plan. The man who sells it to us smells like a bar of soap. "Car salesmen are short," MJ says, "but the men who sell fast cars are tall." Was this true? A young man who smells like he'd been standing next to the first one hands me the paperwork. MJ and her father are in the showroom, circling the windows of an even faster car. I call the bank so they'll approve the purchase on my card. How large a withdrawal will I need approved? "All of it," I say. Her father climbs into the back seat, smiling with teeth: none of us can believe we would do something this stupid. We point it toward the horizon, toward Michigan, why not? When we bring it above a hundred, it feels like we have fewer bones and more blood.

I'm driving so fast I think I hear my skin making noise. MJ yells something about time travel. Her father lies down on his back. "You could!" he shouts. Could what, I ask. "Could fit a lot of sandwiches back here!" He has the wrong eyes. I go faster. We're on our way to see ghosts or goats.

The goats aren't dead when we pull over, just sleeping. "I wanted ghosts," MJ says. Her father takes a walk and becomes therefore very small in the scene, just a poppy seed in a white shirt wondering which film he's in.

From reading books, her father knows it's important to

understand the film he's in. MJ and I look very small to him, like poppy seeds. To him our film is clear to see—it's always easy to tell someone else's film. He knows I've been in one of the hard ones and maybe it's damaged me. The goats got hot and went into the barn, it's getting dark, these kids seem drunk, he thinks. These kids are in a simpler movie than I am, he thinks. The ease of the films of others! To see another person perform their role is beautiful, he thinks. It isn't like one's own film, which is really more of a novel, all the noise and time, what is that, the soul? What a disaster a soul can be, he thinks, what a dumpster. His film, the novel of him, "every person is a failed novel," he remembers Virginia Woolf saying, is hard today. "A year for a normal death, two years if the death is tragic," says a friend over email. Who measures it, he says. He is saying this to his daughter and her grieving suitor, in from Philadelphia, but they are very far away, just poppy seeds. Who measures it? He is saying this to where the goats were: Who times it? He liked it better when he was in the car, on his back, on the way somewhere. He sings the sound of the very fast car's engine harmonizing with the wind, which has the red smell of dirt. He does it unselfconsciously, a boy. He had loved his father, his gentle father, but then without sharing the plan his father died. He hated the drama of it, but he felt a space opening up. He knew he would have to fill this space with love. He knew this would be, as they say, his labor. But not yet. He looked across the entire rust belt to the grieving suitor, just a flea, he'd been walking all this time, and wondered how the suitor had filled his own space with love. How could all that happen to a flea? It was hard to see anything and it was so hot and the goats weren't dead, just resting.

Backseat gurney, MJ's father thinks, on his back watching the corn-blue sky through the sunroof which now they call moonroof. He likes it, how it honors the natural world by framing it. He understands why they put a window in the roof. A window is a guide, he thinks, a kindness. Even the goats had a fence, which seen from above is a type of window. Stay here, says a window or a fence, stay here to look and eat, it's good here. A convertible is too free, he thinks, a convertible pretends to be kind but it's evil, darkly permissive, a convertible is hell on earth. Tell me where it's good, he asks the window in the ceiling, his heart a purse he can't close.

*

To me, my love for MJ was just a fact, unavoidable as any other, no more suspicious than a planet's orbit, which was what it felt like—like I was a rock tethered invisibly to fire.

But the Furies felt differently. They felt I had broken an oath when I fell in love again and they started hunting me, noses to the ground, spluttering snot and blood into the dirt up out of which they'd risen from their horrible sleep to kill me. And there I was: unaware. There I was: in bed with MJ. There I was: "I have no part that isn't yours," MJ said. This was true. Another truth, one neither of us knew, was that there were parts of me that were not hers.

*

We return to the grandparents' house and our experience at the goat farm slides away. It will slide all the way to the pond, I know this, and then it will slide right in—it can never come inside because it was never ours. That's where it goes to become a memory, the pond, which many houses here do have, where it will take its new form and offer itself back to us. I follow it, barefoot, to the edge. I don't want to be inside the house, its countertops barnacled by flowers and foil pans.

I accept the new fur of memory. The goats are bonier than I expected to remember. I picture MJ's father returning from his long walk along the fence to the very fast car. I will make do with what matters most, the barest outline, like a boy under a sheet with eyeholes here and here, I will trust whatever shape memory makes of me, I am its servant whether I know or like knowing. All I am is fur, and fur is all I have.

*

The Furies took literature from me after Noelle died, but I didn't care. I couldn't sit still long enough or be bothered to care about what books could do. So they punished me with a desire to read a specific poem about a rat by my friend Elaine.

Where was the book that held this poem? Somewhere in a box in a storage unit near the green ancestral land where all my and Noelle's things had been moved. I lay in bed until the sun started to rise. I peeked at what parts of MJ had come uncovered in the night and wanted her, really, but not more than how I wanted to push the hair from her forehead and gently kiss her and put on pants and as delicately as I could descend the stairs, trying not to squeak them, and find my car parked a few blocks up Collins and drive an hour to the storage facility where my family had packed up the house Noelle died in and stacked it all up in unit 221, and someone must have put a key to it on my keychain, because there I was, opening it.

Morning sun spotlit everything Noelle and I had ever owned. I knew my mom had been there because it was also beautiful. It was a big unit, double wide, and she had arranged it how our living room had been arranged. There in the center of the unit was our couch, its four legs impressing into the same four indentations in our rug, and draped over its back, there was our blanket, the wool one.

Next to me, a wooden lamp Noelle bought from a thrift store on Morris Street sat on the end table, its cord secreted under the rug, its plug a lump. *Look at what you truly are*, said a blade of sunlight. *Look where you belong but cannot go.*

I started opening boxes. Inside one, I found the book with Elaine's poem "a guest" in it. I flipped through the pages hungry with the desire the Furies had put in me, found the poem, and began reading.

> The rat, sluggish and wary,
> with fur like the dust of the world
> slinked into our street from the sewer
> that edged the corner.

It was chilly in there, but I figured the metal walls would warm up nicely once the sun really got going. Way beyond, I heard cars like waves.

> I knew
> it had come for me. It climbed
> the surface of every door in turn,
> feet spread, attempting entry.
> Confused, out in the open. Yellow door,
> red door, imagining what it had left,
> where next it would be accepted.

I'd read it before, when Noelle was still alive. Probably here on this couch. Noelle might have been on the couch with me, drawing or reading Sherlock Holmes. That is to say, the last time I read "a guest" I probably had a hand somewhere on her body. Where? I don't remember. Maybe later, I'll make it up.

Elaine signed the book to me: "to Michael, elegant ironist," and just like that, I became one. And now, just like that, I became the rat, too. I tore the poem from the book, folded it in half at its waist, then folded that half in thirds, the way a rat might fold a memo. I rolled a little onto my left side and pushed the poem into my right pocket, crumpling it.

I thought about the people in their cars. Heading to work, I guessed. *Do what you love*, I remembered, *and you'll never work a day in your life.* Then I tucked myself under the blanket and slept until unit 221 was so sunbaked I could see it with my eyes closed.

That day lasted more than a year, during which the Furies refined and escalated their punishments and during which most of the events of my little story take place. The poem was the Furies' first punishment, something they wanted me to learn to death. It taught me where my fur came from, why my feet were always spread as I pushed on the yellow door, the red door. It taught me what I had left of my own (nothing) and where next I would be accepted (nowhere).

*

One night before all this, MJ met two gravediggers in a bar. What they told her is you should never sell your land. Land, to them, was the only way to confer meaning on a life. They also told her that due to an old Quaker law, it's legal to have yourself buried on your own land in Pennsylvania. MJ kneed herself onto the bed to tell me. "It's a scandal" is how she began the story. I was asleep and then I was her audience, aquatic, a duck in love, "tell me," I said, "tell me everything," meaning it, lucky.

In Ohio, we're sick of our own thoughts. We're grievers. A few of us go over to the very fast car and behold it in the sun. Others, on the patio, cry leisurely tears. People like having me here. All I have to do is sit here and be seen, and if someone looks at me, I know how to meet their wrong eyes with my own, to meet them in sadness, this is my value and I thrill at it. I thrill to be useful, to remain there without consoling them, as rookies or children would. The platitudes will emerge, as if from the trees. And they are good, even. In the first days, that kind of talk is the bedsheet we need. But when they tire, that's when a windower may arrive, his leg flesh extruding through the patio chair, considering a third beer, not the guide you imagined but the one you have.

The night after the funeral, MJ washes every sheet in the house. It's the kind of house that has everything in supply. I find a wasp alive in a closet. How long is death, I wonder. MJ floats in the pond like debris in the blue light of grief shining up, somehow, from the pond, up into the us of the air, as though it were ordinary, as though it had always been that way, the light tossed up rather than down, the fountain of it we can't notice enough but we try, what do you do when you can't take a picture, the backwards and watery light, the family minus one, how many things can happen in a life, she wonders, floating.

*

What's this, says a voice I have come to recognize as a monk who lives inside of, or perhaps is, me. *A story?*

The woman who became my former therapist told me about him. The monk is on YouTube, she said. He posts lectures about everything and he's got one on suicide.

According to the monk, life is merely a long test and suicide simply an incorrect answer to the question *Should I keep living?* The catastrophe of this wrong answer, he says, has something to do with how it comes at the very end of a life, which encourages the bad habit of reading someone's entire story in relation to their final moment.

I wasn't listening perfectly to the woman who became my former therapist but it didn't matter. I began hearing his questions before she even finished describing him to me.

*

Do you see what you're doing?

Sometimes, yes.

Do you understand you have not yet written about love?

But—

How do you think it looks?

I think it looks like I'm afraid.

Do you know it looks worse than that?

Yes.

Worse how?

Like I'm a dissembler.

And all this time?

All this time I wanted to be a windower, but I'm just a fancy word for liar.

Is that true?

Yes.

Do you know any other truths?

I didn't grieve her right.

How do you know what truth is?

Because when I type it, the sentence of it holds its shape.

What's that mean?

I think a sentence is a form and if it's filled correctly it becomes true no matter what you think of it.

Do you have any other examples of a true sentence?

Noelle would shout one.

What was it?

She would shout, *you ruined my life*.

And do you think that's true?

Depends who's asking.

How about when I ask it?

I think it's true.

But if someone else asked it?

I would lie to them.

Why?

Because I know the answer they want to hear and I think they deserve to hear it.

Why do they want to hear you lie?

They don't. They want it to be true that I don't think I ruined Noelle's life.

Do you think you can make that lie true?

With enough repetition, yes, I do think that.

METAL

Of the two detectives, one has the creepy gentleness of an old cat, and may have been one, but I don't remember him, I only remember the other, who has green neck tattoos, and who sits at our table, which Noelle built, in one of our chairs, which she built also, and asks me questions while my father holds my hand. Her body is upstairs. The people who remove a body arrive separately. Who is this lizard at our table?

That night, my mother sits with me on the couch and asks if there's anything else, anything else, anything else. I spare her no detail. But I don't want to be inside. I sleep in a tent in my parents' yard, my green ancestral land. I don't go home to Philadelphia, not to the table or the chairs, not to any of it, for a long time.

The day after, I drag a chair to the fence of the neighbor's horse pasture. Santiago the dog is under my feet, which are propped on the lowest rung. My brain is on fire—the sheet lightning of sudden loss. I'm hearing every word I know all at once, like a horn the devil is blowing, a nonsense dirge from which I have to spare others by clamping my mouth shut. The horse walks over to gnaw prehistorically on the wood at my feet. It's been ten hours. The funk of an incoming summer rain upturns the leaves. I'm still wearing the clothes I had on when I held her. When I cradled her head. *Noelle is dead she's dead her body turned to garbage*, the horn blares. I keep my mouth shut.

Two days after at dawn, the horse cranes his neck over the fence and snorts through the mesh top of my tent, and I wonder if one snorts *at* someone or *to* someone, and whether a horse is referred to as *one* or by an impersonal pronoun, but then I'm fully awake and remember Noelle is gone and I am not. Something can be so ugly it becomes evil, even a thought.

Three days after, I'm sitting in the front yard of my parents' house, a hilly square of grass looking onto a one-lane road. I'm with two friends, one of whom is famous among the three of us for having recently planted himself a small orchard. My mother, ever respectful of an expert, asks him what kind of trees she might plant in front of her house. "How long do you expect to live?" he asks.

Four days after, I walk up and down my parents' driveway to keep from wondering how it would feel to remove my skin with a gardening fork. I turn off all the lights in the basement and sleep like an animal on top of her clothes, which I'd pulled from their garbage bags (the dead have no luggage), all of it unfolding exactly as in the movies.

When she died, I became the ghost, not her. It will be a long time before I can play some of our music, can bring out a book or two from the storage unit, can imagine a pillow. A long time before I finally donate or throw out most of what we owned, keeping only the books and the records, a final act of cowardice on my part, a silly collector's twitch. A long time before I sell the house and keep the car. I watch TV all day and night, whatever seems worst and most hurtful to people. I prefer boxing.

*

Two weeks after, I decide to take boxing lessons. I feel conspicuous waiting to meet the owner, but the others don't notice me or don't care. He tells me my life is going to change. Punching someone is life-changing, he says. But when I tell him I don't want to punch, I want to *be* punched, the air in the room tilts. He cocks his head in the other direction, as if for balance.

I've said an unexpected thing that revealed something about my body, i.e. a perverted thing. He is listing the equipment I have to buy for my lessons, but his speaking slows until the words become foreign. His body looks young and his face looks old. We both know I won't return.

*

I had fled the so-blue house, fled the city I knew, fled my job, retired myself from every goal. I had insisted on sleeping in my tent on the green ancestral land not for any high-minded reason but because out there I could drink as I liked, crying and making calls, so many calls, and when it finally got late and no one picked up I would put Pharoah Sanders on my phone and sit on the cold ground in my tent like a boy and hold the phone up to my ear as though Pharoah Sanders himself was on the other end telling me something important, which he was—I felt, in other words, that I had nothing and no one left except my mother, and the Furies knew this, and I knew they knew, so I also knew they would eventually take her form.

I believed it was my fault Noelle was dead. I didn't take care of her, didn't love her how she needed, so I had failed. And then I had become failure itself. My mother knew I believed all this. She spent months repeating mantras of protection, sometimes sitting me down and holding my hand, but other times—like the night the Furies got to her, the night I woke her up when I came inside looking for a brick of cheese in the fridge—I exhausted her and she could only repeat the mantras of protection wearily, by rote. Her exhaustion that night is why the Furies were able to take her. I had finally made her weak when I woke her up with my rummaging, my whole head, practically, in the cheese drawer.

*

Three weeks after, I need Noelle's death certificate. I call the state office. I'm told to fill in a form and upload several documents to verify my identity. I do, but my request is denied. I upload different ones: her birth certificate, our shared bank account. Those, too, are denied. On the phone, a confused woman tells me "we don't release death certificates to ex-spouses" and I ask "who would I have to be to get one?" and she says "death certificates can only be released to spouses" and I say "right but I'm her ex-spouse, I am that person, I mean, I would be that person, I would be her spouse" and she gets frustrated: "Ex-spouses don't qualify, sir."

"So if I married her today and then she died, I would qualify?" I ask.

"That's correct, sir."

"But she's dead, so I can't do that. She died."

"Sir, what I'm trying to say is ex-spouses don't qualify."

"Can you tell me in a sentence who is the person that would qualify?"

"Sir?"

"I'm an ex-spouse, so I don't qualify. But I can't understand who would."

"Spouses, sir. Spouses are who qualify."

"That's me, that's what I am. I'm the spouse. We were married."

"No, sir, you are the *ex*-spouse."

"So if she comes back to life and I marry her again but she dies again? Then I can re-upload the forms and qualify?"

"Sir?"

Standing in his kitchen later that day, my lawyer-friend Peter inhales parentally. His kitchen is a perfect square. It has a window at the sink that looks onto a sycamore with some of its bark flaked away, the white-gray meat peering out from beneath. He explains my error. In the box labeled Relationship to Decedent I wrote "ex-husband," but that is not, in fact, who I am. Legally if not stylistically or psychologically, I'm her late husband. I'm not a man requesting the death certificate of a woman I'd been divorced from and who later died. I'm a man whose wife has died, which makes me her late husband, or in other words, her spouse. I made this form-filling error many days before the call. I was wrong before I called.

"It's interesting that you of all people," my new therapist says, "would have made that mistake. And then refused to see it."

That night, Noelle appears in a dream and tells me it is okay to masturbate. Her only such visit.

*

One month after, I make a new friend, Chuck, and because he charms me, I lie about liking metal music. I represent as my own an idea I remember from an article, which is that there is no coherent aesthetic criticism of metal or country music, only classist ones.

When I tell him about Noelle, he lowers his head instinctively, like the conversation is a crawl space. "I know it doesn't matter what I say," he says, which was exactly what I wished people would say. He's a psychologist, so he knows to say it. I am so smitten by his sentence that my heart decides it would say yes to anything he would ever suggest. And that's how I start going to metal concerts.

I stand in their evil blanket of sound and feel, at last, like a whisker. Afterwards, I buy a patch bearing the band's name in a so-serious-it-can't-be-serious font. The patch is always black, the font white or silver, the name is always impossible to make out, and I often don't bother to learn the name of the band. Two months after, we see a band I think is called Armed Ghost, but it turns out they don't even have a name. My favorite part is the middle, by which point I don't know what I am.

*

"We must suffer into truth," says the chorus to Agamemnon in the play that bears his name, after they've overheard his wife stab him in the bathtub.

The myths that are the source material of the tragedies—fathers eating children, children murdering parents, appalling sex crimes, capricious and spiteful gods—are usually understood as symbolic. But that's incorrect. You should think of them as literal.

In one, a daughter is or is not murdered by her father, is or is not replaced at the last moment by a deer (but what about the deer?). It all depends on the version. In the one by Aeschylus, Agamemnon is said to have sacrificed Iphigenia at sea in order to sail on to win the war, returning home to Clytemnestra.

I like the least accurate translations best. What if no one dies, finally, in this one? I've read a dozen *Oresteia*s. But the bodies always pile: most of the house of Atreus, doomed Cassandra . . .

Three months after, Chuck and I see the metal bands Sunn 0))) and Earth perform; Chuck says it's a rare privilege to see them in succession. Sunn 0))) is two men in black hooded cloaks who play down-tuned guitars through plumes of colored smoke. Their music is slow and loud, like God's soundcheck. I can feel my jeans vibrate against my kneecaps and I'm worried I might shit my pants, but I become aware of my body as a specific object occupying space, and that's pleasing.

A few weeks pass. I arrive to the Earth show early and sit nervously at the back bar. Earth is a man and woman, once married. The charisma of the man, who has a belly and holds his guitar somewhat upright, concerns his age, which communicates to the crowd that he has sampled every possible pleasure and suffered every pain. "I have walked through the world's great kitchen," it says. "Now listen to this noise."

Outside, after the show, I find myself in a griever's triangle, the vertex between a widow who became a hemp farmer and a father whose young son has died. One of them is an art historian, or both are, or I am, but the father is my age and has lived in my neighborhood—my and Noelle's neighborhood—as long as I have. The ecstasy of grouping overtakes us. "We're best friends now," he says over his shoulder, walking down the street.

Four months after, Chuck and I see a band called Full of Hell. They take the stage in sneakers, looking athletic and comfortable, like teenagers at a sports camp salad bar. My body registers a threat, so we climb the stairs and look down from the mezzanine rail. The room is dark, small, and flimsy. It seems to me we are about to witness a violent crime, but nothing happens. After a while, Chuck says we have to go. His wife is home alone with their two kids, and he loves them.

Like all my friends, Chuck worries about money. His idea of a greeting is to offer a description of the difference in number between the amount of money he needs and the amount he has. Over time, this anxiety becomes mine, and life comes to seem precarious and desperate. But nobody in any of the thirty-three extant tragedies says a word about money. Money can't help them.

In *The Libation Bearers*, Orestes sets out to avenge his father's murder. Returning from exile in disguise, he arrives to the palace a stranger to his mother and murders her and her lover, his uncle Aegisthus. Hardly anyone in the tragedies gets to be themselves for long: they are disguised or killed. In the *Iliad*, which is better understood as a tragedy than a poem, Dolon is decapitated by Diomedes, who disguises himself in a weasel cap. Worse yet for Dolon, one translator omits the whole scene, thinking it apocryphal.

The evidence for this understanding is that Homer wouldn't have depicted the Greeks behaving so ignobly as to sneak around and kill Dolon at night, away from the brassy white light of the battlefield. As well, Odysseus lies about two horses, which is uncharacteristic.

Poor Dolon, first decapitated, then erased. Here's Aeschylus again: "Better never to have been born, than to live and fare badly."

*

"Look at me," my mother said. I set the cheese down as quietly as I could and turned to face her. "It's not your fault." This was one mantra of protection. "I don't know that, Mom," I said. "You don't need to know it yet. You only need to hear it." This was another. I liked these, but it was this I really needed: "You're going to be okay." It was the only sentence that could save me from the song I was hearing, the lyrics a single question sung by the monk sometimes for hours on end through the night until the moon burned up in the flames of daybreak: *why didn't you love her better?*

The Furies knew my mother's mantras might save me, so they took her from me. She wasn't theirs for long, but for those two seconds a look passed over my mother's face that told me she didn't believe the mantras at all, that she was merely saying some stuff she read on the internet in order to keep me alive, that she had been saying these things out of love rather than truth, and what this meant was that everyone else was lying, too, that every single person who consoled me with their loving platitudes was harboring an open secret, and the open secret was that they knew the truth, and the truth was the rhetorical question the monk was singing to me.

*

A griever knows something others don't. It's like meeting an astronaut who is also a priest. But what they know is distasteful, an accent picked up abroad, knowledge others don't want. Grief confers an honorary degree on this student, who in one heartbeat becomes some kind of mystic squirrel: fuck this squirrel, we think, correctly.

Everyone can feel my sick power. What am I? A windower. Why? Because my wife died. Because I added a letter. What do I do? If I see a dog, I let it bite me. What else do I do? One day, I move all our stuff into the storage company's dumpsters. And what then? Then at last I'm only an idea and I can purr my song because I'm a song, too.

I don't see the hemp farmer or my new best friend again, but there are others. I am identified so often as a fellow griever in the first year that I limit my range of motion to places where I am known by all and places inhospitable to conversation. Every grief is unique, and every griever eventually learns to love his grief, but too much sharing dilutes it, and this is unbearable to the griever, who has no choice but to think of his grief as valuable. Understanding the fungibility of suffering—that it lives in all of us, all the time—and coming to see this as the only necessary lesson of a good life—this is the griever's project. Joy is the final stage of grief, after which follows suffering.

*

When Noelle died (when she decided to die), she made it so I could only have thoughts about her inside the bland compartment of the past tense. She made it so I can only say things *about* her, not *to* her. Is grief what happens when a preposition drifts? It's like if a car got inside you and stayed. Like everything else, its challenges are grammatical: the car, having not been in me once, is in me now.

When we moved to Philadelphia, she started working on a massive sculpture of a half dozen life-sized horses lowering themselves to drink and sinking into water the audience couldn't see. The armatures were pink Styrofoam, the plaster white as a cartoon heaven, each horse was bent differently at the knees, higher or lower, and some were barely visible at all, just the crown of a head and a buoyant mane. She worked in silence I loved hearing. She'd come upstairs to shower off the plaster and we would joke about her Dead and Dying Horses because everything was funny and we would laugh our way through the awful world.

Her talent was outlandish, a strange joke—like she had a virus that rendered her incapable of a wrong or boring idea.

Her prior boyfriends were also artists—the one who nailed a hamburger to the wall, the one who filmed himself washing the professor's car with a bucket of his own piss—and her friends in Philly were, too. At parties, I was a square curiosity. "Can I suck his dick?" her friend asked her, looking at me.

Two of the subheads on the Wikipedia page for "White

Horse" (actually it's styled as "White (horse)") are "Horses that appear white, but are not" and "Why cream is not albino." Nothing, when it comes to white horses, is as it seems. And under "See also," this link: "When a white horse is not a horse."

"When a white horse is not a horse" is an ancient Chinese paradox about the hazard of specificity—adding the adjective makes the first item, *a white horse*, more specific than the second item, *a horse* . . . and a more specific version of a general category shouldn't be confused with the category itself. *A white horse is a white horse*, and *a horse is a horse*, but one should not say *a white horse is a horse.* But who is the person who added this link to the "White (horse)" page, this person whose knowledge begins with the fact that *most white horses are not white* and extends all the way to *and also, those white horses that are white horses are not horses*?

After the horses, she spent a year drawing monks on parade, thin pencil sketches we called Mostly Robes. From enough distance, a group of monks is just fabric. She liked the counterintuitive effect of the robes, which simplify by addition. But the effect of the monks' robes is at odds with the lesson of the Chinese paradox: modification shouldn't be able to complicate and simplify simultaneously.

*

Five months after, a woman has driven my rental car into the center of the field and the field is mud. I'm experiencing a side effect of Lorazepam and alcohol, which means I have fallen into the mud and am stuck there on all fours. The car and I are stuck in the mud. The woman leans on a headlight of the car. There's the woman, her hip on the headlight, which is how I am able to make out her cigarette. *You'd like to join her in that cigarette, wouldn't you*, asks the monk. *You'd like to be inside the car with her rather than outside, in the mud?*

If the widower maneuvers his way out of the mud and into the car, we tolerate his amorousness. But the widower is not to fall in love. The widower who boards a plane to Bangor, drives a rental car into the wilderness, meets a woman and is driven by her into a field where, laughing, she smokes a cigarette and takes in the scene as though it were the most natural thing, as though she belonged there, as though he did: if the widower gets back into that car and falls in love, we may bristle, because he is not yet through being a widower. Widowers are not yet boyfriends or husbands. To say otherwise is to make a category error.

I did get out of the mud and into the car, but I stayed a widower. She drove me to the friend's house I was visiting and I didn't see her again. I washed my clothes and fell in love with MJ a few months later in Los Angeles.

You mean a few months later you made a category error, asks the monk.

*

"There isn't any evidence that talking makes anything better," says the woman who became my former therapist. This is six months after. She teaches me the expression *turtles all the way down*—we google it together, checking she's used it correctly—and the next day I arrive to Ancient Lit with five minutes on the First Cause debate in epistemology.

Turtles all the way down began as an allusion to the World Turtle—the huge turtle whose carapace supports all the Earth and under which is a second, yet larger turtle supporting the first one, and under the second one a yet larger third one, and so on forever. Because I don't want to imagine anything larger than this world, I picture the turtles getting smaller as they go down, rather than larger, but that's bad imagination and poor engineering. The turtles grow ever-wide beneath us. The idea of this turtle stack sickens me.

Later, the expression is picked up by philosophers writing about knowledge: the First Causers, who believe there are foundational truths from which knowledge grows (Aristotle and Aquinas), and much later the phenomenologists, who, like me, can't stomach the image of the progressively larger turtles, thereby coming to think of knowledge as a matter of interacting with what we can see and feel.

Noelle was living in Bushwick when we met, and then she lived with me in Lambertville, and then she moved to Harlem and then Greenpoint while I lived in the Duck Pond, and then she moved to the Duck Pond, and then we moved onto Moyamensing, then Brown, then Rosewood, then we bought the house on Susquehanna where we lived for six years until I came home from New York and found her body, after which I live in the tent, and then I move back to Philly, first to Patrick and Cindy's house near the museum and then 46th, and then 6th, and then Letterly with MJ until we buy the house on Boyer together.

*

Late wife is pretentious, suitable for older, more formal *widowers* (same problem). *Ex-wife* is a lie of omission. *Dead wife* is true but only a lunatic would say that. *My wife, who has died* or even *my ex-wife, who is dead* are factually correct but awkward. One day, in a conversation that requires me to tell a story involving Noelle, I improvise a sentence in the tone of a lecture: *I was married once*, the sentence begins, and I like the soft conceit of this harmless, improvised lecture-sentence, so for months I rely on it, but with time I revise it to *In a previous life I was married*, and then *Life is very long and strange, sometimes*. Eventually, I avoid going anywhere except places where everyone already knows Noelle's story and places where no one will ask for it. Around the second group, I lie about my life. Around the first, I say nothing, unless it seems something is expected of me, and then I say *I'm sorry.*

Seven months after, I fly to Los Angeles after thirteen Januaries with Noelle to learn how to spend one without her. I have hangovers that keep me in bed for two and three days. One night after the next, Mikal picks me up and drives us to the highest elevation in Highland Park, where we eat pizza from the roof of his car. The sun, I hope, will eat my pain, like a tapeworm. I sit on the steps, open my mouth, let it in. That's when MJ comes to visit. I don't want to read, but I change my phone's wallpaper to the picture of Joan Didion leaning on a Corvette, smoking.

A colleague whose husband died corners me in the hall and says, "If I believed in heaven, I would commit suicide."

*

The night I had my head in the fridge, the Furies turned the monk's question into a jelly and then transfused my veins with it. *Why didn't you love her better* flowed through me and weighed me down until I crashed through the kitchen floor into the basement and through the foundation of the house into the ground where the Furies lived and wanted me to live, among the bones and darkness.

Mom peered down into the hole like she hated me. She was dripping blood from her mouth into the hole, like someone had pulled out all her teeth.

"I'm sorry, Geezer," she said, Geezer being what she calls me. "I'm so tired. Stay inside tonight if you can. And try not to eat all that cheese in the manner of a drunk person." Her eyes and body were back to normal.

*

But what happened to Chuck?
He carried me a ways. And then there were others, like a relay.

You used him up, in other words?
In the bathroom at the Misfits concert I told him the band

were the Furies there to kill me. I thought they wanted to kill me for not keeping Noelle safe from herself. Or I thought they wanted to kill me for loving MJ. How they shriek and preen. How they'd love to force a guitar down my throat and open me up and then poke me open with it and suckle the blood from my wounds. And decorate themselves in my blood and put my organs in their mouths, shrieking—this is their labor, Chuck. That's what I said. I said, it's a job and more to them. It's their trade, Chuck, and their calling. Punishment is their métier.

But before you used him up, Chuck knew what to say, didn't he?
The bathroom had a wilderness aspect. It seemed there was piss flying everywhere. There in that scene, Chuck put a hand on my shoulder and said I was very, very sad.

And this pleased you?
Because it was true. Chuck never said an untrue thing to me, which is why I favored him. Others lied.

Why?
To protect themselves from the talk that came out of me, the ever long fabric I pulled from myself like a sick clown.

The monologue of the rat, in other words?
It wasn't Chuck's fault he turned his back on the rat. He had his own life and problems and he barely knew me. He took me to six metal concerts. He always paid. When I got scared at the last one and brought him to the bathroom, he put a hand on my shoulder and said what he said and it worked. It got me through the night. He told me the truth. He did not console me. And he could have done worse. Most of us, soon as we realize it's the rat who's talking, we kill it.

*

We push up to the front, to the bow of the ship, but I forget about the initial violent surge. It gets dark, and I can tell Chuck is shouting the words "Death Comes Ripping," which is the song this feedback predicts, and I'm hit from behind, and my head, like a shoe, breaks my forward fall. Like a meat shoe, like a fruit.

The concussion takes time to become itself. I'm trying to watch football the next day, but all I can do is roll over to face the back of the couch, which Noelle and I bought eleven years before. I use my tongue to fondle the inside of my upper lip, which, to use the lingo, is split. I feel a teenager's private gleeful pride about my injuries. Glenn Danzig is sixty-seven. The song is one minute and fifty-three seconds—a cloud of razors.

"Rip your back out," he sings, "and death comes ripping out." The concussion doesn't teach me anything. I eat a bag of grapes.

THE VOLCANO

"It's like putting a volcano sticker on every page of a book called *The Volcano* and writing about the trajectories of ferries leading to and from islands where volcanoes erupt but not once mentioning volcanoes," says Taije, who knows what I don't want to mention.

"I don't understand your shame for loving MJ or what the fuck you think you were supposed to do. You were what, thirty-five when Noelle died? Were you supposed to never love again? What the fuck," says Fady, who doesn't.

"You're in that moment right before puking," says MJ, who does.

The monk, who sometimes knows what I don't want to mention and sometimes doesn't, clears his throat.

*

I email Mikal, asking him whether I should write about the affair. When he writes back, I open it, but I'm not ready to decide whether to include this story in my story. I click on "mark as unread," returning his email to bold.

When you do this, when you mark as unread, the preview displays the first email in the thread. Which means for weeks whenever I check my email I see my own question, plaintive, lowercase, and clipped off:

i know i will never be free unless

*

Weeks after the affair ends and I tell Noelle, one friend hugs me and says, "What did she expect?" This is a person who knows all about the marriage. But another friend who also knows about the marriage calls me and says, "You've lost your fucking mind." The affair is brief and intense and consists of four long walks and one night in bed.

Because I'm a boy who doesn't know anything, I repeat a single fact about the affair over and over in the salvage months, in the yelling months. It has the loophole-feel of something a lawyer might intone in the final moment of a closing argument, and I say it often with none of the embarrassment I feel now, as I type it: "I never got hard with her."

But Noelle won't ever believe this. "Tell me you got hard or I'll break this glass on your face," she says, but the thing is, I can't say it. It isn't true. I never got hard with her. Noelle stands up and brings the glass down against my face.

"It doesn't even sound like an affair to me," says the woman who became my former therapist. "It sounds like you took some walks with a pretty girl."

"There are cases where the punishment doesn't fit the crime," says my new therapist who reads no literature.

"Rest in peace, sweet Noelle," says the subject line of an anonymous email sent to me six days after Noelle died. The body of the email has two sentences. The first one is, "I hope you're happy." And the second: "A pox on your soul, you piece of shit." This was my first Fury, and because it had no name, it became everyone.

A friend who knows all about the marriage suggests a chapter on the bad part of it, the part that came after the good part and prior to the affair, to provide context for the affair. Context for the context. But I don't want to do too much of that.

I decide once and for all I'll write a short chapter called "The Volcano" confessing to the affair and contextualizing the abject shame that was decomposing inside my grief during the year my book describes.

Do you want credit for breaking your silence, asks the monk.

*

Noelle had just turned thirty-five. The internet said that was when you had to have a serious talk about children. The internet said many confusing things about Noelle's health.

Then she turned thirty-six. What did the internet say about thirty-six, I wondered, but I was too scared to look it up.

I knew what I wanted: to have this life with her, just us, wine and movies and not many friends but it was enough for me, it really was. But then another life directly after this one, a completely different one. The day I realized this I sat on the bed in a towel and stared at the radiator and wept. Noelle didn't come upstairs to check on me. I don't know why she didn't check on me.

"I told you from the beginning I didn't want kids," she said. I remembered and also didn't remember her telling me this from the beginning. It felt like something my ancestors knew—like something a ghost had told me. Like maybe it spooked me and my soul deleted it. I knew and I didn't. It was a fact about my wife I put out to pasture.

She asked over and over would I leave her just to have a baby with someone else and what if we tried and she just couldn't, would I punish her for trying but failing and how would that sound, she asked, when people found out. I didn't know the answers to these questions. I was living full-time in the numb field with a fact about my wife. I was alone with a fact.

"You ruined my life," she said again and again and no variety of apology could touch her feeling. She felt that I had broken something on a whim—a whim is what it was to her. This feeling was so hot it melted whatever I offered it.

At night I tucked the sheet around the couch cushions. In the morning I folded it up, dropped it to the floor, pushed it back under the couch with my foot. I would make coffee so quietly the coffee never even knew what was happening. I went to work.

*

If I tell you it was May when my new friend and I talked about what had been happening and I asked if I should kiss her and then did, and I shook from nerves and sadness and desire, and if I tell you I believe the number of times I saw her, for walks and picnics and to kiss, was four, and that we spent a night together one weekend when I had left home for a few days to stay in my friend's empty house and that we got drunk and did not have sex but slept there, in the manner of an old married couple, and if I say I remember putting my phone in my jacket pocket and leaving it in the living room . . . If I say I told Noelle about it and then spent a year filling up the so-blue house with language about it, if I say after a year of that language drowning us Noelle was killed by herself and then, somehow, six months after, I met MJ, if I say all this (I fell for my new friend but never fucked her but my wife died in the circumstances raised by what led to the not-fucking and also by that not-fucking itself, if I say I then met MJ and did fuck her, sometimes whimsically and sometimes apocalyptically, and the manner of the fucking, I believe, caused us to fall in love more or less immediately, stunning us and those near to us), if I say all this then I believe I have finally emptied myself of every rotten detail and can maybe go on.

Except: there are details my friends and family carry for me, details I have erased. Except: whatever Noelle wrote on the sign on the bathroom door, the red sign. My parents know what it said but I have not asked. Except: Taije says when she was cleaning the so-blue house one day a few months after, she found a popsicle stick with something written on it and I have not asked what. Except: Suzanne knows what record was on the record player and I have not asked what it was—it would have been muffled, vibrating up from the first floor to the bathroom. Except: after I told Noelle I let her take an X-acto blade to my dick and make a small cut. There, that's it now.

*

My new friend sends me pictures of goats. The marriage is almost over, I say to myself. What's the harm. These are just pictures of goats. She tells me about an abandoned pier and says we should go see it. She'll bring beer. The landscape is murky, rotten. Mud on your new sneakers, a stink on your work shirt. She sat on my lap and pulled on what hair I have. That's all.

That night, I push the sheet back under the couch and then, when I wake up, I go to work.

Later, Noelle stood up and brought the glass down against my nose. We both cried for a long time after that and then I wrapped the sheet around the couch cushions. I tried to fall asleep to a podcast. I tried every trick I knew.

*

A year later, Mikal proposed to Tiffany in New York and wanted to celebrate. Noelle didn't want to go and she didn't want me to go either, but the woman who became my former therapist told me it had been over a year since the pretty girl, and I had to return to normal. I said I was going and we fought, we filled up the so-blue house with language. She was treating a headache with an ice pack and when I kissed her goodbye on the top of her head I kissed mostly ice pack and then I walked out the door and sometime later that night she took her silences upstairs into the bathroom and made them permanent.

SERTIG PATH

Nine months after, I'm waiting for Taije on the Rocky steps. I always have so much gum in my pockets, some of it chewed. The world feels like a toaster I've been dropped into. It's like I've been buried, alive and upright, inside a tree. Insights are flickering but I don't own them any more than I own my own spit. Taije is the only friend I want to see, Taije who is capable of any thought and sometimes many at once, in bursts.

We decide to get a drink before looking at art. The bartender is wearing all black—it's Yogev, my star student who once saw a Fury, and I think, Yogev could do anything, and probably will, and he could be anywhere, and probably is.

The music in the bar sounds like rainwater pushing through chimes. Yogev's bar—Noelle would not have liked it. It's too expensive, too marbled, too many suits. Finishing my third drink I feel swaddled in an opulence she would have found unsavory. Then I feel bad, like I ruined a date with a ghost.

Then I feel bad for ordering a third round from Yogev, who slides a book across the bar for me to look at, but I don't care about the book and I don't care about Yogev. "Yogev is a type of ghost," I say to Taije.

We're supposed to go to the museum to see the Bruce Nauman room. It was my idea. It was Noelle's idea. The Nauman room is something she would have liked and I'm still chewing through the months of grief when I'm doing things for her, alone or with a proxy. I'm taking a ghost on dates, sometimes becoming one myself in the process and sometimes inadvertently whisking the ghost of Noelle into the body of a friend-proxy. I'm like a driver hit by another car. I'm careening but I think I'm steering. The Nauman room is a video installation of the artist walking but the walking, as you sometimes have to say to students, is more than just walking.

I don't care about Bruce Nauman. I sip what Yogev made and drink the chime water and want to drown.

I don't remember how much I knew about art before Noelle. It feels like my ideas about it were always mine, but I know that can't be true. Marriage is an exchange of clouds, and it's difficult to sort it all out when it's over. Her ideas came to feel correct over time and eventually the whole cloud of them settled in my cloud. She thought, for example, that Duchamp was worth puzzling over. I did too. I came to despise him, but it took time for that.

*

Noelle's friends dressed in old clothes and were usually on drugs, a pack of six young Rod Stewarts I called in my head the Labradors. They were beautiful. They floated and spoke all at once and drank interchangeably from whichever beer was closest and from time to time they fucked one another. One night, smoking outside a diner that was also a bar, a Labrador in gold Nike high tops vomited in the moonlight and then led me by the hand to the bathroom where he showed me how to take cocaine. I liked it, but not as much he did.

They DJed at the neighborhood bar: psychedelic rock and gospel, all of it old. Their favorite band was Spiritualized, who play droning psychedelic gospel music about taking heroin, led by a singer who calls himself Spaceman and plays from a bench, stage left, wearing shimmering silver pants, and requires a music stand from which he reads his lyrics.

Walking toward the kitchen at a party one night, I overheard Noelle bragging to one of the Labradors that I had just published a poem. She repeated the name of the magazine, casting a spell. It was one of the few that sounded impressive to the general public. She was proud of me. I came around the corner and saw her sitting against the refrigerator, her friend leaning on the counter. Everyone in the house but me looked like they were in the Byrds. "Tell her it's true," Noelle said, and I raised my eyebrows to confirm it. Her friend looked at me as if she were appraising an owl.

That summer I was learning Noelle's Philadelphia—how to walk to the movies through the old cemetery; the Chinese takeout with the butterfly collection on the wall; the TLA staff picks; the 700 Club and Standard Tap; Bikram Yoga; AKA. Is love just proper nouns? She worked on her horses while I wrote poems upstairs. If I finished one I would fold it up and try to slide it down the banister. I kept a journal about what we ate and drank. I thought I might publish it one day.

"I forget to spin the lettuce, I forget to drain the beans, I forget to screw on the pickle lid, I forget to strain the pasta. We go upstairs and play the Chopin record so loud, do it like sixteen-year-olds, then lie in bed and listen to the voices on the street."

Her Philadelphia was smaller than I expected, and by the end of our first summer there, it shrank to exclude the Labradors. Except for one, who appeared at the front of the room on the first day of my poetry writing class, chewing gum in a jean jacket, and wrote the most beautiful poems. But the semester ended, and I didn't see her after that. Years after we lost touch, Spiritualized played Radio City and I spotted a Labrador at the urinals. We walked together to the bar, where he passed me a plastic glass of cheap champagne over the head of a stranger. That was the last time I saw any of them.

We listened to Yo La Tengo's "Autumn Sweater." We watched her beloved Herzog films. We drank beer in Vermont, where I proposed.

We flew to California and eloped in the desert. Simon's kung fu teacher married us and then we went to Hawaii for our honeymoon and rented a house on a flower farm. The owner of the house showed up late one night with a machete to kill a centipede that had bitten me on the foot. Noelle was working at an auction house but got laid off. She started teaching Bikram Yoga and we bought a house in the neighborhood where the Labradors once lived, what they call a workman's rowhouse, three rooms downstairs and three up. It was built in the 1890s and had been in one family, a collapsing gem with inlaid floors and bad wiring, six hundred square feet on the first floor and four hundred on the second, a bathroom so small it threatened to disappear. The family's name was listed as Buck, but welding tools in the basement were labeled Bukowski. The sellers didn't attend the closing. Their agent didn't know if Charles Bukowski ever lived in our new house.

"These houses are old, Michael, someone's died in all of them," the realtor says years later when I ask if Noelle's death should be disclosed. Noelle's fires, the smoke that killed her, the wine she took with her to the bathroom for courage. The market is bullish. None of it takes long.

*

Taije and I climb the Rocky steps again. On the way to the Nauman room, I see a painting I've never noticed.

It shows a mountain in the middle distance, a cabin in the foreground to the left, and two people walking a path that winds down the middle of the canvas, through the valley. Everything looks natural—this is how a tree looks, and a cabin, and people from a distance, and this is how they all fit together—except for a few details. The undersides of some of the pine branches are done in haphazard flecks of brown. And if you follow the brown flecks up the tree line to the left, they point more or less to the sky, in which you'll find four green clouds. And beneath the clouds a bulbous, purple mountain peak, unlike any to be found in the Alps, which is where the scene takes place, I learned later.

I felt chosen by this painting, and I desired it. Where was Taije? Probably in the Nauman room by now. I wondered how many other proxies Noelle's ghost was directing and where they were.

Compressed into a feeling, the paragraph of your grief can outlive just about anything. It lives in you like an ocean, mouthful after mouthful. No one knows what else to do but drink it. You swallow the water and swallow it. Everyone you meet is a different type of fool who wants you to stop drinking the ocean. The only not-fools I know are Taije and the painting, so I sit down on the floor and she joins me. "I can't sleep with you," she says. I squint at the topmost dimple in the purple mountain, then open my eyes wide and take in the whole painting, unfixing my gaze until the colors run together, a broken stereogram. I have the freedom of grief, the whole ocean of it. "Can we stay here?" I ask.

*

On pay-as-you-can Sundays at the museum Noelle and I used to sit on the Rocky steps with coffee and then pay $1 to sit in the Duchamp room. *With Hidden Noise* was the one she liked best, a ball of twine held between two brass plates by long screws, in the center of which Duchamp had a friend place an object—no one knows what it is. "I don't know if it's a diamond," Duchamp said, "or a coin."

She liked wearing brown boots that came up to her knee and she liked them to be Frye. She liked to tuck her jeans into those boots. She liked having bangs. She liked having blue eyes. She liked sitting on the Rocky steps and she liked sitting on the bench in the Duchamp room and she liked asking me what I thought was inside that ball of twine. The knuckle of a mouse, I would say. Tiny ice cube in a tiny freezer, I would say. Then she would tilt her head onto my shoulder, which she liked doing.

Is Duchamp a metaphor, asks the monk.

Do you think Noelle faked her orgasms, he asks.

Her favorites were Miro and Duchamp, one hot and one cold. I don't think you should be able to like them both, but it seems most people who like one also like the other. I can't shake the feeling that Duchamp hated the world and its people. Miro is who I prefer. Miro makes me feel better.

It's stupid to think this way, but anything helpful must also be at least a little true: I wish her heart had tilted toward

Miro, toward a warmer future, every red a homecoming, meaninglessness fashioned into a bright light, some lines on a canvas, a comfort, some limes on a campus.

What are you hiding from?
Let me say it how I want. I'm the one who held her body, not you.

*

I don't really like museums. Only one time, when a student asked "are these all real" and I felt useful and maybe even good for having brought his class there—that time I liked it. But I don't like how people act in museums. Everyone in a museum is quietly bored, or pretentious, or out of place and feeling stupid. I especially dislike new museums. I don't like not knowing how to get from one room of art to the next like I do in Philadelphia. I can get you from the suits of armor to Twombly quick, never doubling back, and I don't even like Twombly. My friends can tell you so much about the Twomblys, many of them composed with the humble pencil. All I can tell you is there's a small Kurt Schwitters assemblage hung just outside the Twombly room, and it's good to pause there before you turn the corner. I always pause there. I'm always bringing students to see the Twombly room when we read the *Iliad*, the gigantic aggressive Twomblys purporting to tell the story of the war but who can say? Students always want to know was Twombly crazy. Of course he was crazy. Even though I don't like museums or Twombly, I ask them to meet me there often. I want them to see me move through the building, an expert at being there. At walking through the long halls happily, joking with security guards, tipping the coat check, disinterest for the impressionists, at ease in culture's loose pocket, warmed by it, open to its warmth but not reduced by it . . .

This, in other words: "I wanted them to see what it would feel like to feel powerful in the classroom," said my friend when I asked her why "eating a sandwich at the front of the room, and taking my time at it" counted as a lesson.

*

Why aren't you writing about Sertig Path*?*

Because I was looking at pictures of Noelle. Because I have remembered some things I tried to forget. Because I searched her name on my computer and found a picture of her death certificate and she will never be older than thirty-nine. Because I remembered something we used to call Stick Wine and I remembered Vermont and I remembered when her dad died and I had never seen her cry like that. I had gone back to her parents' house and fallen asleep and she came home from the hospital in the middle of the night and stood in the doorway and I put my arms around her and she put her face in my armpit and she cried and shook and it was so dark I could only smell her and feel the soft imprint of her nose. Because I am remembering later that winter she got pregnant, our second year of dating. And she had an abortion and spent all night in the bathtub and every so often I would go in and add more hot water for her and sit on the bathroom floor with my arms around my legs and I didn't know anything, I remember not knowing anything. And I remember she talked to the pain she was in. She didn't talk to me. She talked to the pain. She said "I understand what you need" and she called the pain "honey" because she called everyone that, that and "sweetie," which always surprised me because nothing else about her suggested she might want to call someone that. And another thing, instead of "goodbye" she always said "so long," which I once heard her say to David Byrne when he was leaving the gallery in New York where she was working when we first met. He was holding a horse-riding helmet under one arm and rolling his bike with the other. And when he complimented the gallery she said something to him she later told me was a Talking Heads reference, "it's a multipurpose space," and then he squinted his eyes and smiled and tilted his head to one side because she had just revealed one percent of herself and thereby indicated an entire galaxy lived inside her. "Did he get the joke?" I asked later and she said "Michael he's David Byrne yes he got it" and kissed me. That night we celebrated how Noelle quoted David Byrne to David Byrne and made him smile and by the time we got back to her apartment we had to pee at the same time so she said "you sit first and start / and then I'll sit on you / and pee between your legs" and it was such a brilliant, efficient system but she peed all over my thighs and jeans and because the super left the radiators on full blast, the bathroom window was open and the cold air rushing in through it was in an argument with the radiator, which was screeching and whistling and clanking its retorts. And then we collapsed in bed with some of each other's pee on us. A few months after her father died and after the abortion I found a plastic grocery bag full of empty vodka bottles hidden in a closet and when I asked her about it she said "those are from before" and I said "are you okay" and she said "of course I'm okay" and looked at me like I was a boy who had never heard of anything and I said "are there any more of these plastic bags full of vodka bottles" and she said "no" and I hugged her because I was a boy who had never heard of anything, and she put her nose in my armpit for a while and I rocked us side to side.

Is it really true you could feel her nose, asks the monk.
It is. I think it is. I think it was.

*

Taije strolls in and together we behold *Sertig Path*. She seems to understand right away what's going on with me. One of her tricks. How long do we stay there beholding? How many days is it since Noelle died on the bathroom floor? How many since the day after, when I came home from Mikal's engagement party where we ate Shake Shack and drank champagne in Brooklyn Bridge Park and then I went home and broke open the door to her discarded self?

"She's been gone for a while," the EMT said blankly to me or to his colleague. I was surprised they hadn't run in. Cool as cucumbers up the stairs and then back down. And then two regular cops, and then two detectives. Then Joe, who was closest. Then Suzanne, who would have been closest but was at a party. Then my family: mother father sister, in that order. "I can't believe she had the guts," someone said to me years later. I was taken outside while they brought her body down and out the door. I remember the body bag coming down the stairs, its precariousness, but I know that's not possible because I wasn't there. I was outside when they brought her down. I was outside, my back to the fence and my knees to my chest, because my family thought that was best. But somehow I see the body bag clearest of all. Later, my father collected the rose petals and grills from the bathroom, and bagged them too, and these bags I was permitted to see coming down the stairs. By then they had brought me back into the house, maybe because it was hot and humid out. Maybe those bags are the ones I remember. Where was Santiago the dog, who saw her go upstairs but not come down? Then we all left. I guess someone went around turning off lights. My sister drove me in my car toward the green ancestral land and I never went back to that house. Kurt called and said "I love you, Michael," which sounded strange to me. Brian was there when we arrived, on the land where my family once grew their soybeans. Others were on their way. It got dark and it was raining. My father and Brian put on raincoats and walked down the long driveway holding lanterns—I didn't know my family to own lanterns—to help others find the house. I was in a spare bedroom with Suzanne, side by side on the edge of the bed. "This is going to get worse," she said. It had been six hours. Others arrived, on and off for months. "I'm fucked," I said, and my mother said "No you aren't," which response lived in my body for many years, waiting.

*

I gave Noelle my number on a piece of cardboard I'd found in the bar. Our first date was at the gallery, an opening for the performance artist whose specialty was taping himself, high up, to the wall. I remember smoothing a long piece of it across one thigh and over his dick and balls to the other side and then across his opposite thigh and then down the thigh into the crease it made with the wall, and I remember that was the moment his body felt most like a corpse to me. By the end (it took hours and a team of us), he was suspended ten feet in the air, a mummy on the wall. We left openings for his mouth and nose, our corpse-friend Santiago Something or Other the performance artist. He'd done it many times before. He'd even taped himself to the front of an eighteen-wheeler once. But when he wanted to come down, and he struggled under the accretive pressure of the tape to say "scissors" and I returned with regular ones he said, "surgical," which I could barely make out from the pressure of the tape across his chest and neck and everywhere else.

What he meant, he told us later, is we needed surgical scissors because regular ones wouldn't cut the tape we'd used but what they would cut was his body. Noelle said go and I pushed open the overlarge gallery door and looked out onto Hudson Street. I knew something I didn't know I knew. It was a secret knowledge blooming inside me: that Santiago would suffocate if we didn't get him off the wall soon.

I ran to a pharmacy, ran back. We cut him out. He stank and his feet were wet. No one knew whose fault it was we didn't have surgical scissors. Santiago the near-corpse toweled off in the center of the scrum of spectators and pulled on a pair of sweatpants. The audience was acting like this was all part of the performance. They had drinks in their hands.

Later, we decided Santiago liked that moment—the moment when a twenty-two-year-old on a first date had to save his life—and the best way he knew how to create that moment was to encourage it by not overplanning. By not packing surgical scissors. The moment he didn't pack surgical scissors made a negative space my running filled. He was improvising ahead of time, conjuring me, predicting a friendship. I ran fast, his performance bounding out of the gallery inside me and down Hudson Street.

Santiago trusted me before we met, and that's why we named our dog after him. Now it's fourteen years later, Santiago the dog at my feet.

My little story is short: she left me here to watch our dog die, too.

Is this still the performance, asks the monk.

Why have you still not written about Sertig Path*?*

Because there's a part of the story that is . . . not quite believable.

Oh?

Something separate from how the painting made me feel.

What was the feeling it gave you?

Peace.

But that isn't the not quite believable part?

No, that's the boring part.

Oh?

The not quite believable part is something I learned about the artist way after. A biographical fact of his life I learned after all the times I stood there beholding *Sertig Path*, chewing my gum and crying and feeling peace. It was the only place I could bear to be alone.

And then?

And then they deaccessioned it.

Took it down, in other words?

Took it down, its purples and oranges like chewed gum on the underlip of a desk. I stood there a long time in the gallery where it used to be, alone and chewing. I never knew they could do that, take a painting down.

What did they put in its place?

I don't remember. Art. They put art in its place. At first I thought I was just in the wrong room. Eventually I gave up. I went home and looked it up and bought a poster of it. I remember I sat at my shitty desk and shook and cried.

And that's when you encountered the not quite believable part?

I found out why he was painting those mountains. They're in the Swiss Alps. Davos. He'd been sent to a sanatorium, which can be spelled with an *o* or an *a* in its third syllable, and later to a cabin among the larches—those spindly trees he painted ever so near to realistically.

Shall I sing my questions now?

I don't care.

From what was he healing dear Michael dear Michael from what was he healing dear Michael from what?
They called it a nervous breakdown. He was suicidal and mountain air was supposed to be the cure. This is where he made the painting, lonely and healing.

Lonely and healing?
And the grace of those two states was offered to me when I stood before it. It was very unsubtle. Its force was brute. One of the larches, for instance, has a curve in its trunk about halfway up, and where it curves, the trunk goes pink, like it has a belly. This is how he saw the tree. He let me see it how he saw it. I returned, I returned, I returned. But at the time? I didn't know his story. I didn't know anything. I don't think I believed in knowing. I don't think I believed in belief.

But when they took it down, you learned all this?
Yes.

And he carved his own chairs, didn't he?
Yes.

Just like Noelle?

Just like Noelle.

Shaved and whittled and formed the things that held his body?

Shaved and whittled and formed.

And after many years painting the larches, he died—as we nowadays say—by suicide?

I don't know when or where or how.

And you still have the poster?

I am flattening it right here, next to my shitty desk. I have four books pressing it down, one on each corner.

And for how many years have you been flattening it?

Many years. Six or more.

Will you ever hang it?

I have plans to hang it, but the plans disappoint me.

Because you still think about the real painting, don't you?

I say thank you to it.

And this is the not quite believable part?
It is.

Would you like to say it now?
Thank you, painting.

*

A few months after our first date, the gallery was rented out for a horse race afterparty. The owner asked Noelle to sleep in the attic and keep an eye out. We packed a bag. On the subway she laid her head on my shoulder. Her right leg, crossed over her left, bounced when the train bounced on the tracks. She hooked her foot inside my calf.

Behind the front desk was a panel in the ceiling with an access ladder, which we climbed to the attic and then drew back toward us, shutting it ceremonially. The attic had a couch and TV, a plywood floor, a few lamps from Ikea. We sipped whiskey from tumblers we borrowed from the party. The equestrians didn't give us any trouble. We watched a movie, tangled ourselves on the couch, and slept. In the morning we pushed open the huge gallery door and stepped into the white light.

If we took a minute to watch the Sunday traffic and smoke, it would have been Parliament Lights with the recessed filters, and we would have done this up the street, near the corner of Hudson and Spring, in front of the deli after we got coffee. If we didn't stand there, as we often did, smoking and watching drivers miss the turn for the tunnel, I wish we had.

MONSTER

Ten months after, a hurricane floods the basement of my parents' house. I'm in boots, water to my knees, when Noelle's small library of gardening books floats by. My father hands me a Ziploc baggie with the jewelry she was wearing when I found her. My phone's algorithm compiles an album it calls FUN MEMORIES and pushes a thousand pictures of Noelle to my home screen while I'm teaching Aeschylus. I recognize the apron as hers. I recognize the shirt Suzanne's daughter is wearing. I recognize her butt in jeans downtown. I move through the days gingerly. I learn to soften my eyes.

On my way to MJ's, trying to remember the facts about myself, I hear the monk's questions. I wish it were otherwise, but I know it could be worse, too. *What if it rains*, he asks. *Do you have a rain plan for this walk? Who gave you all this fur? Do you know you can't have MJ? Do you know* can't *is not even the best word for it? Do you know the best word for it is* shouldn't*?*

I get lost in front of her apartment, dissolved in the black night, beamed around the corner. She gets my text and opens the door but I'm not there. Did he ever even exist, she wonders. But she feels certain I was real—no one would have imagined such a person, a drunk with an eraser for a brain who slept in a tent in his parents' yard and cried in his sleep. She finds me a few blocks away on the steps of St. Michael's, playing songs by Meek Mill on my phone, scratching Lotto cards with a stranger. It's so late and dark here in the center of God's belly, "too dark and late to worry," I say. "We're safe here, as safe as safe can be, safe as church mice, actually," I say. Then she touches me and I change into a playing card so she can slide me back into the deck, where I'm even safer.

*

Would you like to light the burn pile with your father and watch it, the monk asks in the morning. *Both of you sitting on five-gallon buckets in the yard, thinking of all the cold beer you'll drink later, June breeze adjusting the gnats, your father again reminding you—loudly, over the sound of the flames and the song—that Kris Kristofferson was not only a Rhodes Scholar but also a captain in the Army, and you telling your joke again ("Kris Kristofferson: half bad actor, half bad singer, all bad ass"), the fire rising to the status of metaphor in real time?*

I do want all that, so I drive home to my parents' house to sit in the yard and watch a fire. What I really want is every tattoo. Sunlight on the trees, sunlight on the tires. I want to feel like a letter pulled from its envelope. I drive up the driveway, keep going up the hill into the yard, and put it in park at the top, where I pitch the tent. When is the sunlight most real, before it hits the grass or after?

My father brings the radio into the yard, sets it down in the grass by our feet. I can tell there's not enough here to warrant a fire, not yet, but he's humoring me, he's loving me, we're going to burn what we have—a few wagonloads of old leaves collected from the gulley down by the street and a few tree branches that came down in a storm. It's not much but it's ours. It lights up fast. Waylon Jennings sings about how dangerous he is in love.

I say something I half-remember about birds mistaking

highways for the rivers they follow as migratory flyways. "They get lost above our highways," I say, "and tired, and the confusion can kill them." We look it up and Google suggests people like me are also likely to ask a question I hadn't considered: "What does it mean when birds are flying everywhere?"

It suggests an answer, too: "They announce prosperity, progress, and abundance coming into your life." Symbolism is a stupid way of seeing the world even if we all come around to it eventually.

When Noelle scattered her rose petals before she died. When I did, years earlier, before she said yes when I proposed. And when my father tilted the dustpan of them into a garbage bag, not once but many times; she plucked the rose bush nearly bare, probably in the dark.

Why are the petals a symbol but not the garbage bag, the monk asks.

I move slower and slower through the world, careful not to wish for symbols, aware that I do.

What kind of person writes beautifully about suicide, the monk asks.

A monster. Which is what I will be if this works, meaning the best I can hope for is to fail.

But you don't really want to fail, do you?

*

The house Noelle and I bought was so blue on the inside it made you seasick. It was so quiet, so blue—our neighbor to the left was in jail for selling pills, and the house to the right was vacant. It was a narrow little sea.

A year after she died, I tell the couple who buys the so-blue house to keep anything they like that is still there, including the bookshelves, which they do in fact like. Now I keep my books in the basement of a new house, in boxes stacked at the foot of the stairs. It's difficult to find any particular book because my rummaging over time has randomized the contents of every box: each has three columns of books, and in the remaining four-inch space, another six or seven books can be crammed in haphazardly. But I like the college library feel of it, going downstairs in socks with a book in mind I know I won't find, spending a few hours emptying out boxes and refilling them differently, putting in a load of laundry. Once I found a receipt from 1998 inside *The Tennis Court Oath*—that experience would have been weakened by sunlight, I'm sure of it. Upstairs, one must ask oneself how the past got there, but in the basement, the past is tactile, like a tire swing.

A year and a month after, I'm having dinner with a married couple who keep books by living writers downstairs and dead ones upstairs. When I ask them how it feels to carry a stack of books by a recently deceased writer into their bedroom, they tell me with their eyes I have derailed the conversation. There's a deep practicality at the core of their system: with too many books for either floor of their house, but also too many of any one genre to split them that way, the only way to split their two lives of shared reading was on the one hinge that matters, the little dash between the two years that tells our story best.

No one knew what do with the contents of the so-blue house after Noelle died. It was decided that I—I suppose I was the primary remaining content—should be taken to my parents' house. But as for what remained behind, no one knew what to do. Unlike the books of a writer you've never met, when your wife dies, you can't just carry all her things into your bedroom, although most grievers at some point on their hell-ride will try. Eventually, an embassy of friends went to the house and transported its contents, whole, into storage unit 221, which I would then visit, in hopes that consulting with the stuff of our life might help me to know something.

Why did you stay in unit 221 so long that day?
Something about the way Noelle's foot wrapped around my calf that day on the train.

On your way to the gallery for the horse race afterparty?
The way it hooked it there. It fit. No one can tell me why this memory is so strong, why it wheels me into the emptiness behind my little story. Her foot felt like it grew there, as my father says of a particularly snug fit between two pieces of wood cut to size. And I loved how it felt like her foot grew

there. But now that feeling is distant, like a news story in a foreign country.

Would you like to quote the Rilke line?
It feels far and long gone by.

And?
That's all the Rilke I know.

Rilke was Rodin's secretary, wasn't he?
I guess.

Do you remember when Noelle brought you to the Rodin Museum?
Of course I do.

And she showed you The Gates of Hell *out front?*
It's only a reproduction. It's not the real one.

Do you understand my question?
Maybe.

Did she hook her foot around your calf on the bench in front of The Gates of Hell*?*

I can't remember. I remember the couch. I remember we fit nicely on it. For a long time I thought all our objects held meaning and if I kept them, their meanings together would black out the universe. So I tried to get rid of everything to make a new life possible. But when I found it impossible to get rid of everything, when objects kept resurfacing, I had to learn that some things can bear many meanings over a life.

Have you fucked MJ on this couch?
I believe so, yes. I believe we have fucked each other on this couch, is how I would put it.

And you find the meaning of this couch bearable? This couch on which you and Noelle once fit nicely and on which you and MJ have fucked each other?
A couch can bear a lot. That's what I learned. I think a couch is like a ship and meanings attach themselves like barnacles as it sails. I feared these barnacles but then I didn't. Maybe a couch is like one of the deeper-down turtles in the stack, very wide and strong for meaning. Maybe a couch is like a forgiving parent. It gave me comfort to learn this. I became less afraid.

*

A year and two months after, I read an article about mushrooms. Then I take mushrooms. Something floats into the corner of the bedroom. It hovers there so we can speak, one song to another. I feel the bedroom widen, the lungs of the ceiling expand. It turns out grief is just a shapeless gray thing, a dead muscle, not the full animal I thought it was. I look at it a long time. I want to touch it. I've ridden it hard, haven't I? I leave it there in the bedroom so it can leave or die, but what it does is reconstitute and force itself back on me. It will do this over and over.

*

On weekend mornings like today, my father walks across the driveway to the garage and turns on the Outlaw Country station on his satellite radio. Then he drives to the deli to buy a coffee while the songs play on quietly, unwinding themselves for nobody, sometimes all day and into the night. Then, when my mother nudges him, he'll walk back out to turn it down and shut the garage door. People who write sad songs, sad poems, sad books, what's their idea? People who write their sad sentence all day and deep into the night to nobody, what happens when they finally finish reheating the meal of their sadness?

To write your sentence, first you need a garage. It doesn't have to be yours, but it needs a radio. Turn it on, then decide you want a coffee . . .

. . . She made her smoke with charcoal she piled inside a small grill she bought (according to her bank statement) that day, having placed it in the bathtub, leaving Santiago the dog downstairs alone to shit everywhere, which shit helped me to know without knowing as soon as I saw it, and I ran upstairs to the bathroom door, which was duct-taped shut and had a sign on it that I will never remember except that it said CAUTION or WARNING in red Sharpie, the door being locked from the inside, Noelle having locked it and stayed there, lighting her fires, lighting her fires in her nice dress and her expensive necklace, having sprinkled rose petals too, choices which, since she left no note, were her final words to me: a dress I loved, a necklace I bought for her, and an allusion to our engagement, where I scattered rose petals, all of it not just a terror but animal, an animal terror in our little house where now a young couple who at settlement seemed fearful in the ordinary way will live their lives for a while, which lives will involve in part a bathroom with a new doorknob because I broke it off to get in, that summer—

"Everyone asks me how she did it," MJ says. "The worst are the ones who think they're kind." It's normal, though, people wanting to know. It's normal if you wanted to hear the sentence.

Would you like to hear my *sentence*, asks the monk.

People don't ask about her life, and that's okay, too. They don't ask about how private she was, like there was a sheet wrapped around her soul. They don't ask if there was a name for that sheet or if there was a person who gave it to her or told her she needed it to be safe. They don't ask about our marriage. They never ask about our marriage. Asking about the marriage would be crazy. And they don't ask if I expect to have a normal life even though Noelle twirled her sheet into a noose.

I said, would you like to hear my *sentence*, asks the monk.

*

A year and three months after, the semester is winding down. Classically speaking, a catastrophe is an act of destruction so final and utter it requires a God to appear, dangled from a crane, to figure it all out. The expression is *deus ex machina*. "Don't think of 'machine,'" I say in class, "well it does mean that, 'god from the machine,' the machine being the crane, but I always think of 'mechanic.' And I always think of *ex* not as 'in' but 'as.' *God as mechanic.* These gods are weary, and their weariness makes them like wizened mechanics, pulling on giant cigarettes, leaning on the garage wall, wondering what idiot problem is about to roll in. They're immortal, but the price for all that time is to spend it forever intervening in the lives of fools."

When Noelle died, I became a catastrophizer. Another word for the person who acts like this is a Cassandra, who was right and knew it. If you only like one color, everything matches. My black house, my black outfit, my black breath …

Tragic characters know things they wish they didn't, or they don't know things they wish they did, but I can't think of one who expresses a known fact happily.

In class, we've reached the end of the little story of Orestes for the fourth and final time. "It's good to know the plot as well as you do," I say to the class. "The original audience knew the plot ahead of time, too. For us, when Athena cranes down into the action at the end of *The Eumenides*, it's easy to groan, easy to be ironic. But I like to think about technology, about tragedy itself as a kind of technology. If you have the tools to build a crane, you'll probably use those tools and build that crane, and if you have a technology called writing, and you apply that technology to a thing called plot, and you bend that plot into a tragedy, and you're wondering how to conclude that plot, you'll look around for a technology to help and boom, you'll lower a God down from that crane to tie up loose ends. Actually that crane is the precursor to our boom truck, which is how you get, for example, something like a pallet of drywall through a third-story window. I take it you would not snicker at the operator of the boom truck, or at the pallet of drywall? You would not think of them as benighted contrivances? When the Gods come down in their machines, it's true and actual." I'm surprised to say this.

I hate the cheap trick of etymology so I never mention that the word "tragedy" means "goat song," either for the animal skins the actors wore or the prize given.

"So Athena's been called down to break up a hung jury who can't decide whether to turn Orestes over to the Furies or grant him sanctuary in Athens. The Furies have pursued Orestes all the way to Athens, and their plans for him seem to include devouring him whole, taking so much of his blood into their mouths as to choke a mortal: 'From you I would / win nourishment to make a human gag,' says one. The best arguments from Clytemnestra, appearing here in ghost form, are not enough: 'Orestes wins, even if the votes are evenly cast,' Athena says, forsaking the murdered mother and sending the Furies into apoplexy. 'My breath is rage and I am total wrath,' says one of them. The audience already knows. They woke up knowing. But if the Furies can't be appeased they'll terrorize Athens forever, so Athena has to think of something. What does she have? The Furies are older than she is, but she has a special technology. You can see where this is going? She may not have the clout to strongarm the Furies, but what if she offered them a new position in the company? What if these Furies . . . what if we called them, Athena says, Eumenides instead? Eumenides, i.e. 'the kindly ones,' the first major rebranding effort in the western world. 'Boom,' Athena says, 'you're kind now.' The standard line is that these colossal bloodthirsty snake-haired murderous hell-birds made of ooze have been transformed into gentle ambassadors for the new city of Athens by the magical force of language. But here's what I really want to say. In the final moments before the transformation, look how much deep feeling Aeschylus has for the Furies, who live 'dishonored beneath / the earth, loathed and despised,' and remember this is the part of their song that repeats, they're the chorus after all, and this chorus is a sad gang of forsaken primal deities, they're universally reviled and they know it, they woke up knowing it, they themselves are haunted: 'What is this pain that penetrates my heart?' asks one, mirroring Orestes' speech earlier. This is to say: for Aeschylus, even these frightful monsters are subject to the sick jacket of despair—call it fate, or life, or time itself. Toward the end of the negotiation, just before the

Furies accept her offer, look what Athena promises them, the promise that seals the deal: a life 'completely free from grief.' Such is the force of the perfect offer, that it slides the jacket right off you."

*

My new therapist hasn't read the tragedies and I don't think she cares to. She works in the Gestalt mode, which means she's waiting for me to admit I don't trust her because she hasn't read enough literature, but I won't, ever. With her, I can bend the myths and blow into them like a rubber glove, inflate their fingers into the air-sausages I prefer.

Are you finally ready to hear it, the monk asks.

Monster,

he says, which is not a sentence but a word, and not a kind one.

*

A year and four months after, MJ puts on Neil Young, but it was Noelle who taught me to love him—her favorite was *Tonight's the Night*. One morning early on, Noelle decided we should buy it. Her apartment was an unrenovated deli with a meat case running through the middle, no bedroom windows, no shower, just a chair in front of the industrial kitchen sink.

She didn't own much, but she had a good job at the art gallery, so when she decided we should listen to *Tonight's the Night*, we just went to the record store and bought it, and then went to the electronics store on Bedford and bought a cheap all-in-one record player, and then some lunch, and then went home to the deli to play it.

She knew what she liked. And whenever she revealed something she liked, it was like a fox had leaned in to whisper me a line of Shakespeare. We played that record for thirteen years.

Now if I so much as think of a song we used to love, the

thought itself feels hot. In the time it took me to open the bathroom door and find her, not just songs but the entire map of our life shattered inside me. No one can help me understand these grief fevers, but I can touch their heat until I teach myself not to.

*

My father and I atop our buckets remembering the nicknames of George Jones: "Possum" and "No-Show Jones," for how he looked and for his propensity to get drunk and miss his own concerts, respectively. My father stands up and walks towards the garage but returns on the mower, a bunch of old cabinets towering in the cart he's pulling. He puts it in park and looks over his shoulder to see if my mother is looking, and then, one by one, we lower the cabinets onto the flames. We tell each other the story about the time George's brother-in-law hid the car keys to keep him from going to the liquor store, so he drove the mower instead. Telling the story together, a chorus of two, audience of flame, a hundred feet of hose at our feet in case it gets aggressive. The hose, I mean, permits us to let the fire aggress.

Monster, says the monk.

You have to tell your stories carefully. You have to know when to stop. You can't drape a thousand blankets of your dread onto a person, the miles-long snake of your hell-story, formless and outside time, without hurting them. Talking is the air on which early love is supposed to travel. I was sometimes a punisher, perhaps a monster, in that breeze.

Her voice is like syrup coming through a keyhole. "I'm not afraid to hear it," she says about Noelle's story, and this is another time someone says a thing I had been hoping to hear.

I tell her I had worried Noelle would kill herself but that I didn't worry enough, and I tell her how that black fact had settled in me, a tumor. I tell her the tumor had a valve that the Furies were pushing air through. I tell her the woman who became my former therapist wanted me to believe certain things that I did not want to believe: "suicide is a homicidal act directed inward." I tell her the most odious of these ideas was the possibility that Noelle had wanted to set me free.

*

She takes me out back behind the rowhouse, into the postage stamp backyard. This is what she's wearing: an oversized black cashmere sweater she took from the lost and found at the restaurant where she works. I'm shifting and shifting in a mostly broken yard chair. Wood becoming not a chair. Or a chair becoming merely wood under me, shifting. It can't be true, as I have often thought, that I loved her from that very moment. What I loved was between eight and ten milligrams of Lorazepam every twenty-four hours and talking. Preferably to her, which is what's happening here in the postage stamp yard.

She listens to my sentences about Noelle again. She has heard them so many times over the phone but never in person. She stands up, drags her chair closer. "Come here," she says, and takes my head between her hands. The syrup of her voice opiates me. The postage stamp yard is let's say ten feet wide by five deep, a different style of fence along each side. There's a dog at my feet, a nice dog. I realize the dog is cold and then I realize I'm cold.

Why are you here, asks the monk.
Because I'm allowed to fall in love with her.

Why is that?
Because people fall in love. Sad people fall in love.

Are you sure?
No. I've never known anyone as sad as me or as partial, like God shaved me down with a knife. But there remains a sliver who likes to be in love.

With this woman? The one with her hands on either side of your head?
With her, yes.

But this is melodramatic, isn't it? The holding of your head?
It feels good. I like it. It feels good to have one's head held like this.

Her hands are stretched open, like my head is a soccer ball she's preparing to throw. I'm leaning in slightly, to help her keep her grip. She has been looking at me for one, two, and three seconds. Then she says it. She says what I remember.

"You're okay," she says.

The dog at my feet is not mine but he's cold. Her sweater ripples like a flag. The sky is cold. It keeps getting bluer and colder and it has no birds in it or planes. Her roommate steps out into the yard with her boyfriend, a veterinary student in black Chucks and white hair.

Is this our new family, asks the monk.

Am I falling in love with MJ because of what she just said? Or am I just happy on Lorazepam?

I said, is this our new family?

In the near future: the roommate will find me asleep on the kitchen floor, a frozen pizza blackening in the oven. In the near future: my rat snoring will force MJ to ask me to sleep on a cot in a closet at the other end of the hall. I slide down the hall late at night and climb into the cot and watch basketball on my phone. There are so many rolls of toilet paper in there. That night is the first time I hear the question. I hear the boyfriend or the roommate in the bathroom, and I worry they might open up my closet for a spare roll.

Why are you here is the question. *Isn't this all a little embarrassing* is the question. And: *Surely she knows*?

"I don't know where I am" is the answer. And in the ways that matter I don't know who I'm talking to. I think I'm picking fights with MJ, who at some point becomes my new girlfriend who buys a cot and asks me to sleep on it. The fights feel soupy, hallucinatory, irrelevant. I start them and lose interest. I walk away not in anger but forgetfulness. Never once does this life-altering sentence occur to me: "I don't know who she is."

It doesn't occur to me because it isn't quite true. I do know who she is. But I want her to be Noelle, too. Noelle was killed by her worst part, like her mirror's reflection became a murderer. But what about the rest of her—the good rest of her? Why would I want to say goodbye to all that? So when MJ wasn't the good rest of Noelle I would hate her for it and sulk in the closet and I would stay up all night watching basketball on my phone, I would prove I didn't snore by not sleeping and then I would drive woozily back to the green ancestral land at dawn, making as much noise as I could leaving, and I would wrap myself in blankets and walk over to the tree where my whiskey was hidden in a hole and drink a little and then climb back into my tent and then I would snore like the rat I was and this, I am telling the monk, was how my soul was processing my love for MJ. This was my process.

*

Her hair is long and black. She wears the roundest glasses, the reddest lip. Her glasses seem to surprise her face. I remember those months when no one looked how I expected, when everyone was more beautiful. Anyone alive. "You're so beautiful," I'd say, "so beautiful when you watch Jeopardy / make waffles / look at your phones / sip wine."

I call her from my tent. I call her from the rock I like to stand on. It's early November and then it's mid-November. She tells me she is sitting in bed and she tells me she is trying to lock her bike. She laughs and tells me I'm not the first sad guy she's ever loved but I am the saddest, and I ask, "but am I the most inept?" and she says, "you're the most inept, Michael."

"I need you to fuck the blood out of me," she says.

What's this, asks the monk, *what's the big idea?* He's walking away from the rock into the woods. I know he expects me to follow. *Are you serious*, he says, *are you seriously*, but then all I can hear is the zippering and unzippering of my feet grinding leaves into pulp. I feel the ecstasy of the call sliding away. The trees have winked off their leaves; now their branches look like fried neurons. *What's this*, asks the monk again.

She calls me from her yard pinching the phone against her shoulder and I hear the wind flipping its picture book. It's November, then December. She sends me a dirty text from an airplane bathroom on her way home for Christmas. *What the fuck* says the monk *is wrong with you?*

By then it's too cold to sleep outside. "I know it sounds dramatic," I say, "but a house is a reminder, houses have bodies." Can a man live inside a phone, I wonder. Inside a voice. Inside the stories early love blows in on. "Tell me," we say to each other. "Tell me tell me." She tells me her friends are nervous. And her father. "Are you sure," he had said to her. "Are you sure you know the size of this thing?"

I'm only a tape unfurling its noise, benign, or so I think—whatever you think you are is what makes you a danger in love. I'll learn to see myself differently but that takes time, which goes tick and tock.

*

I remember I couldn't drive slowly enough and cars were honking for all different reasons and I heard Noelle's laughter and I saw her right hip, it had dipped just below the roofline. I remember the pocket of her jeans like that. Maybe a rivet catching some sun. She had climbed halfway out the window trying to push down the fin with her body, cracking up—she squinted when she laughed hard.

For her monks, Noelle wanted Masonite as a drawing board—at Home Depot they cut a sheet in half and we roped the two halves to the roof of the car inexpertly, so the front edge transformed in the headwind immediately into a fin. And that's why I remember Noelle's right hip through the windshield. It was like she was consoling a shark out there, waving with her free hand to the other cars.

I was laughing too. We got it home, five miles an hour the whole way up Moyamensing. She cut it into smaller pieces, one of which was the size of a clipboard, and that was the one she brought with her to Hawaii years later, to the flower farm. I think she chose the flower farm because she wanted to draw there. I think she planned to sit in the yard, drink wine, and make some drawings of monks in the gardenia and under the birds of paradise. Hawaii suited her. She liked the beach, she liked her red tank top and her cut-off jeans and she liked gathering things for dinner slowly from different farm stands, greens in a tote bag like hair, and she'd usually pick out one extravagance and it was usually cheese. There she is now, smiling.

She liked the yard. She sat out there day after day before and after we went to the beach, looking out into the flowers. I think she was deciding how to draw the monks in relation to the flowers, whether the monks should be very large or very small in comparison to the flowers, which were out of this world, vibrant beyond what you need. She'd put something low and slow on the stove, or eggplant in the oven, peppers in the oven—it was close to the French doors to the yard, and some of it would waft out to meet us in the flowers, you could leave everything open, there was no difference.

But one day she stopped bringing her Masonite board out into the yard. She made up names for all the animals passing by—I don't think there was a duck but there may have been one. There was, I'm sure, a dog, some cats, a few goats. She was trying to make up good names for the animals. She wasn't trying to figure out the monks. She was trying to sit in the yard and look at it. After the day she didn't bring out her Masonite board, she kept on not bringing it out. It was like she was practicing not making art, and she got very good at it. She got very good at sitting still and not making art. I don't know exactly how good she got at looking, but I think she got *really* good at it. If you ask me, I will tell you there came a time when Noelle could see every single thing.

*

I don't remember it, but MJ says I downgraded our first date from dinner to sitting in the park and then all the way down to me showing up at her apartment with three bottles of wine in an overnight bag. Close to midnight I came to her door and she was waiting on the stoop. It had been six months since Noelle, and "since Noelle" was how I was saying it back then, passing over the "died" or "killed herself."

Years later, the euphemism "died by suicide" comes into favor. I dislike it on the grounds that it's too easy to say: "Noelle died by suicide" doesn't hurt me to say or type—the balming effect of the euphemism makes it too easy on me. The sentence I currently prefer is: "Noelle was killed by herself."

At a kid's birthday party, a married couple I know comes through the door. They see me, and then MJ, and raise their eyebrows innocently, like they'd remembered something embarrassing. I know what math they're doing. They're figuring out how many months it's been between Noelle's death in May and today, a cold day in November when I showed up with this beautiful woman dressed as if for a date. *Why did you even bring her*, asks the monk.

I'm at the snack table when the Furies make me gigantic. My face is so wide I can't hide my shame anywhere. It's as wide as a movie screen. The Furies don't stop. They manage to shrink down everyone else. I can tell the whole party, a dozen or so parents and their even smaller children, suspect I have something to do with it, and they aren't wrong. *Do you understand how well they can see you*, asks the monk.

I get down on all fours, my back grazing the ceiling. I feel their eyes on me. "He's gained some weight and she won't last," I feel them thinking.

I'm worried MJ isn't dressed right for a kid's party. I'm worried she's dressed exactly the way you'd expect. *How can you even manage a thought at this size*, the monk asks, and then I think, let's get out of here. Tiny MJ is chirping something from her tiny red mouth: "are you with me," she asks. "Are you here with me right now?"

Just then, I remember something: smokers can excuse themselves at any moment and everyone understands. All we need to do is hold our cigarettes up in the air and jiggle them. If we could get out of here, I figure, things might go back to normal. So with my right hand I sweep tiny MJ into my left. I cup my left hand and she tumbles down the slope of my fingers into my palm.

I raise her up and hold my arm out so we can see each other face to face. "The Furies shrunk down everyone but me, whom they enlarged," I say. "But they forgot I'm a smoker."

"I'll smoke with you," she says. All I have to do is find a way to fit through the door, which is the size of my fist. Still on all fours, holding MJ loosely in my left hand, I balance on my left elbow and with some unsteadiness manage to turn the doorknob between the middle finger and thumb of my right hand. I can see outside to the normal-sized and gray November world outside the house. I try to squeeze my head through the door, first straight-on and then by turning it to the side, offering the doorway my left temple first and then rotating my head slowly as if it were an overstuffed chair being delivered, but to no avail. So that I don't crush tiny MJ, I set her down at the threshold. She scampers out.

"Maybe I should go feet first," I think, my feet being narrower than my head. I can see MJ is already smoking on the sidewalk, erotic and regular-sized. So I start a K-turn there on the living room floor, taking great care not to crush the Furies—the last thing I need is to squish them into my flesh where they would do God knows what to me from the inside. I move my right knee and right hand backwards just a touch, then use the leverage of my right hand to gently propel my left side forward and I keep at it like this, alternating—it's slow going, but soon enough I'm facing the room, and then I reverse-crawl, right and then left and then right and then left, until I can feel the cold air outside drifting up my pant leg, and I know I'm close. I start to work my huge right foot through the door, twisting it this way and that, thinking the smallest thoughts. I can smell MJ's smoke wafting in. There on all fours, blocking out what little winter sunlight might otherwise have been permitted through the open door, I take in the scene the Furies have made.

Do you know what else crawls around on all fours, asks the monk.
No, I say, lying.

Do you need a hint?
No, I say.

Would you like to fuck your red-mouthed girlfriend in the car, he asks.
I would, I would.

Later that night, she asks how I got out. We're laughing. There's no law against it, then or now. There in the car of her bed, laughing, I bring down her underwear.

*

These were the early circumstances in which eventually, later, not in her backyard in Philly but when I was in Los Angeles and she came to visit and we drove to Venice Beach, I fell in love with MJ, and she with me. But first, she brought us from the stoop through the breezeway to her backyard. I have no memory of the three bottles of wine, the overnight bag, or having moved the date. I only have what she tells me. I don't remember showing up so late. Actually, I remember arriving in daylight—I remember seeing her for the first time in the daylight—but this is wrong. I remember noticing a witchy quality about her, but this, too, is wrong. When she finally held my head between her hands and said I was okay, I remember the row of potted plants on a rickety bench behind her, but I'm afraid to find out if this is right or wrong. I only know the bench is real because it's in the basement now with the wolf crickets, who live down there, on the prowl for moisture.

Then it's January, the new year. I make a right at the bottom of the driveway of my parents' house and I make a left back onto it, up into the green ancestral land, and in between I'm with MJ. I go to Los Angeles. I'm trying to pick up Lorazepam. I'm having trouble. I'm in a plastic lawn chair in the plastic lawn chair aisle of a CVS, sunlight pressing obscenely against the long windows behind the cashier. MJ flies out to pull me from the lawn chair, and that's when we fall in love.

She's here with me, here in the CVS. She looked it up, she called the Uber. She's who shovels me into the back seat and then pets the webby flesh between my left index finger and thumb as we ride under the palms, Muppet heads on spikes.

I remember how she rocks backwards to pull on her boots, the chill of the sand on the beach, I remember *On the Beach*, I don't remember how we get there or when we leave, only how she tilts backwards onto her tailbone, straightening one leg up into the air to slide on the boot. "Do it like this," she would say later, repositioning us.

It's March and then it's April. She jumps up from a deep sleep when Martin Sheen is thrown from the rooftop like meat. Now she's awake, so we go for a walk. *How do you prefer the moonlight*, asks the monk. I can hear the sidewalk under us: right on Sergeant, right on Frankford, right on Huntington, and back to Collins. I see the streetlights, their feet tucked into the concrete, and whatever people finished and dropped to the ground or tossed from their windows is being whisked by the breeze. *Would you like to see the garbage fly*, asks the monk. *Is the reason you'd like to see the garbage fly because it's ugly*, he asks. *Why do you crave this garbage hurricane*, he asks. *Where do you suppose Noelle is Where do you suppose Noelle is Where do you suppose Noelle is Where do you suppose Noelle is Where do you suppose Noelle is Where do you suppose Noelle is Where do you suppose Noelle is Where do you suppose Noelle is Where do you suppose Noelle is Where do you suppose Noelle is Where do you suppose Noelle is Where do you suppose Noelle is Where do you suppose Noelle is Where do you suppose Noelle is*

"Oh," sings the chorus in *The Libation Bearers*, "when will it finish its work?"

*

MJ's apartment on Collins is near the so-blue house. I remember with some embarrassment how Noelle's ambulance blocked traffic and spun its lights through everyone's windows, a Sunday morning, and I hope no neighbors will see me here. Not the young Christian couple who tied a white rose to the doorknob the day after and not any of the others. I only want to see MJ, even though it sometimes makes me feel awful to see her. Could I have said that to her? Would it have been good for us if I did? Some Mountain Dew bottles roll around like claves in love on the sidewalk.

I guess it feels awful in an ordinary way. Guilt, like grief, is ordinary and fungible. I think it's located somewhere specific in the brain, in the spine. Its voice is the monk's: *You shouldn't be here*, which he revises into a question: *Can't you see it's wrong to be here?*

People say trauma is time travel and it is, and I'm afraid there's nothing interesting to say about it. I can always hear the siren of Noelle's ambulance and feel the scratch in my throat from how I screamed.

I see MJ walking toward me. I don't know what do with this love, or how to think about it, or if it's wrong, or why it's happening. *How does she do that with her scarf*, asks the monk. She is singing quietly to whatever is playing in her earbuds. She is headed straight for me, under a line of low trees, but she hasn't seen me yet. I look at her and feel something paint over all my thoughts in a single stroke. Maybe it would take time, but I promise I will let this feeling burn away the guilt. I promise I will let myself be in love with her. The promise feels simple and good, like I'd caught my balance on an icy sidewalk. I stand up when she sees me, a little bit formal, and watch her walk toward me. I remember when my mom saw her picture and said, with something like concern, "she's very beautiful, sweetie."

What is she doing here, asks the monk. *What's her problem?*

She has black hair she wears up. She likes a red lip. I will learn much later she has a fondness for contemporary country music. This will baffle me.

Do you understand the difference between them, he asks.

Not always.

It's like the first time we had a fight. I lost track of a conversation and tried to bluff my way back in—*is she still talking*, the monk asked, alerting me—but it was obvious what I was doing and I didn't yet know I could just cop to it. We fought. I said something awful, something about how she is—demanding and over-sure—and she thew her hands up and looked up at the ceiling. "Do you think I like being this way," she asked. That's when I fell in love, not on Venice Beach, and not at the CVS like I said.

You can love someone merely for their sentences. Merely for the surprise of what they say. For how their sentences inflate the world like a balloon. And so—

*

I still have my legs and they get me all the way back to Collins. It's hard for me to rejoin the conversation; it's ongoing. And the monk is ongoing. *Is that conversation ongoing*, he asks. He's laughing.

JOAN DIDION

I happen upon a criticism of the book I'm reading, something the book doesn't do, and when I return to it all I can do is wait for the book to reveal its inability to do this one thing. I've killed it.

I don't actually care what the book does, I just wanted to read it. I drink a tequila and think of movies. I only wanted to read the book, but then I encountered the book-killing essay, and here we are, vulnerable to essays, real losers.

I drink a tequila, I think of different movies, I feed the cat whenever she wants. I think of my friends and family, the TV passwords we share.

I'm trying to read the book by Joan Didion, which is canonical in the genre and which I resisted all this time. My friends have ways of determining why a book is bad, but I almost always like a book and finish it. I know there are bad books in the world, poorly written and affected, but I don't seem to come across them.

When I read a book the only assumption I make is that I'm in love with the writer. I read a book pick my nose drink a tequila on ice with lime, *clink* goes my finger in my nose when the drink is empty.

Until my early twenties I assumed every book was self-help, which was why I liked books even though I hadn't read many. They helped. They helped the self. But this was, as they say, a misapprehension, which college can be good for adjusting. Books were all sorts of things, hardly ever self-help. There were such things as self-help books but you shouldn't read them. In fact there is no self, a fact which you had to learn from books. Now I was twenty-one, twenty-two.

One thing I didn't know until today is that Joan Didion actually wrote two grief memoirs, which is a way of saying I didn't know she experienced two tragic bereavements, first of her husband (*The Year of Magical Thinking*) and then of her daughter (*Blue Nights*). I resisted the first because I wanted to write my own; the second I didn't technically resist, unless not knowing is a resistance, and maybe it is.

I googled the Joan Didion Corvette picture but I googled badly and came across the book-killing criticism. I don't mean the criticism is correct, necessarily. What I mean is I started reading in order to reach the place of my inevitable disappointment.

I guess it's thrilling to say what's wrong with Joan Didion on the internet. I could have disregarded the criticism, but that's not the type of reader I am. I'm trusting. I used to think it was crazy how easily my classmates knew a writer was wrong or stupid, what the writer overlooked, didn't have the guts to say, or was ignorant of. Almost every writer, it turned out, is wrong and stupid. It was thrilling for me. At some point in class, usually the first five minutes, somebody would begin to enumerate complaints, and by the end, we had really degraded the book, pulled the pages out, made them frail, noticed how frail and shit-smelling they truly were, foul, and above all, stupid. I was twenty-four, twenty-five.

"You aren't ready to say that," I say to my students, which they don't like hearing. Classrooms are where teachers struggle to become the parents of their students' ideas. I'm just begging them to slow down. "Why do you dislike everything?" I'll say to no one in particular. "You're like my old classmates. Can someone please just tell me what's happening without criticizing it?"

"Please," I say, by leaning myself dejectedly against the door frame. I'm forty, forty-one.

I'd done so well resisting the Joan Didion book, but then I gave in and started reading it, and then I googled badly and killed it. One, two, three, four.

*

Her account of life in the year after her husband's death has much in it that is familiar and true to me. It's easy to see why a book like hers would be self-helpful to others: a book is a device that extrudes thoughts and experiences compellingly. I'm not against criticism, it just isn't my first language. When

I read criticism, I feel like I did in Italy, where I struggled to order even a cappuccino, MJ behind me, laughing. When I couldn't remember the word for eggs in the market, I improvised *frutti del pollo.* This was Sicily. The map they gave us showed the neighborhood laid out in the shape of a dick. Who are the world's great map critics?

It was thrilling to watch MJ order and ascertain Italian things. Erotic in the sense that she had something I didn't. "Show me how you make the wine appear," I said again and again.

We stood in the Greek theater of Syracuse on a cold morning, beset by limestone. Mostly I was bored, thinking of sex. I took pictures of the different parts of the theater, taking care to get the very blue sky in each shot. "I'll show my students," I said, but I never did.

One night she sat down at a piano in an empty room of a type of place called a *baglio*, and thinking she was alone there, played a version of "Can't Help Falling in Love" so delicate and tender that I, lurking behind one of the building's many stone walls, began to weep as though something evil were forcing itself out of my body, and I thought, this is why everyone falls out of love, this is why old people have no friends, because as you age it all becomes too much, love itself if you get lucky and are permitted to face it squarely has a light you cannot bear, if you see your love singing like this and know she is singing about you it will be terrible and you will beg for it to stop.

*

I am learning to say something, to say it unqualified: I loved Noelle and now I love MJ.

And now I can see this book is the lozenge of the sentence I work and work in my mouth, learning it.

I see MJ and Taije together, drinking and fierce and intense, and I love them. I see Mikal and Simon together at the zoo and the animals make us sad and we wish we never went, and I love them. I see MJ and Mikal together when he visits us and I love them. I see Simon and Zach together for a reason I can't remember, and I want to rub both their shaved heads but do not, and I love them. I see my mother and my wine expert friend and we drink wine on the patio on the green ancestral land and I love them. I have a dream where the woman who became my former therapist sits under a pink tree with my new one and in the dream I never existed, and I love them. I see MJ with everyone. I see her ride Taije's bike down 8th Street to where we parked and come back with jackets but all she has for Taije is a bedsheet which without flinching Taije fashions into a huge scarf and returns to her cocktail and I love them.

*

Who is saying what to whom and why is what I ask my students. Cautiously, over the din of their criticisms. When Noelle died, I took a leave. I went to Los Angeles. When I returned, I felt like a bag of spiders. A good reason to resist the canon is the likelihood that Joan Didion already said it, *a bag of spiders*—

But who can live on a diet of masterpieces, said my old teacher. I think of Taije's husband, the strangest person I know, who somehow managed to publish a book of new ideas about *Hamlet*.

As I was finishing *The Year of Magical Thinking*, I was trying to remember my own time in Los Angeles, and I thought looking at the picture might help. I knew I would never be able to find my copy of her collected essays, the one with the famous Corvette picture on the cover. It was down in the basement in a box, as good as gone. So I googled it, but googled badly, and that's how I came across the criticism.

In Los Angeles there was a little back stoop behind the apartment where I would smoke in the mornings. There was always broken glass back there I didn't want to be blamed for. It seemed to me some kids were probably tossing beer bottles over the fence into the tiny yard, carpeting it in broken glass over time. I remember standing up from the stoop and walking over to the plastic lawn chair, and I remember sitting down and doing something dramatic, which was googling the famous picture of Joan Didion. I had to brush the broken glass off the chair. I had never read a book or even an essay by Joan Didion at the time, but I associated her with Los Angeles. I hand-swept the broken glass and behaved dramatically. The pizza on the roof of Mikal's car—was that dramatic, too? I made the famous Corvette portrait my phone's wallpaper. Every morning there was more glass, more glass.

I said Joan Didion said she felt like a bag of spiders to you because it's thrilling to lie. It's hard to remember what happens, how it's all said, and sometimes you pick up later on the page than where you left off. Imagine those gaps. Joan Didion may have written things you skipped or had thoughts she didn't write. How would you know? How did you get a new idea about Joan Didion, I want to ask the critic. How did you find something missing inside of what's already mostly gone? You're the strangest person. I love you.

*

Her book ends with a story about swimming with her late husband at Portuguese Bend. He's less fearful about timing it than she is—you had to time the swell as it rushed into this little cave. "You had to feel the swell change," she says.

Readers extrude the book when they read it. They empty out the cave by their reading and later their experiences are the swell that fills it back up. If they misremember the book by conflating it with their lives, so too did the author, whose stories themselves are a mixture of books and life. When we read, what are we getting closer to?

In the early months of bereavement, Joan Didion and I couldn't read. We were all life, no books. We report crosswords (for her) and boxing on TV (for me) as replacements for books. We refused life.

The desire to read, to extrude—to settle scores. Read poetry at speed, prose slowly, said my old teacher. A good book, like a good exam question, should include all the punctuation marks. It gives you a feeling outside your body, like a neighbor's orgasm on a plane.

But my point is that *The Year of Magical Thinking* was organizing my thoughts before I read it. It advertised a method of grief, and it was influential to me even if I hadn't encountered it. I'm not sure how this works but I believe it.

We call this faith. "I believe because it is absurd," as someone said. I picture all the other books I haven't read, how they steer me.

To put it simply, the world knocked me around until my behavior came to resemble the methods for living that books like Joan Didion's promoted. Then I climbed into Joan Didion's pocket and saw things even more clearly, which is what Tolstoy, who was talking about books a person *has* read, called *an infection*. "The stronger the infection, the better is the art as art," he said.

I hadn't read the book but I had been triangulated toward it. Then I read it, after resisting it, and when I read it, I realized I hadn't needed to—I was already in the pocket, the book was good but redundant with my methods for living.

*

If narration had a timestamp, we couldn't love it. Narration is supposed to concern itself with time but it should sidestep it, too. It has a cloud-aspect to it, like a cloud that talks. And when it passes, each one it passes goes, "ah." And because of all this, it relieves us of our own thoughts, it puts them on ice, it decapitates and steers us.

The difference between consciousness and narration is insubstantial. A narrator is just a figure who can make all their thoughts, including the worst, give pleasure. It's easy to see where the instinct to narrate a horror comes from, but we should go backwards first.

Almost immediately when it happens you start forgetting. And whatever you forget is where narration will go later. "Memories are what you no longer want to remember," is how Joan Didion puts it, which probably means that the memories that remain are often too painful to bear, but she also seems to understand narration requires the gaps, and memory is the enemy of gaps.

We lift the horror out of time and arrange it, misting a cloud-aspect into the gaps of memory, like exterminators. We become loved.

*

"You never cried around me," says MJ. "But your eyes were always glass. You were lazy and wild, tiptoeing around the fringes."

"Around the fringes of what?" I ask.

"You knew something, but you wouldn't tell us what. You just told me to wait. That if I waited you could love me."

"Did you wait long?" I ask.

*

Aphrodite, it turns out, was the sister of the Furies. What happened is her brother Chronos cut off their father's testicles and threw them into the Mediterranean. She was born in the sea foam that rose up when the testicles splashed in. Meanwhile, back on land, Uranus left behind many droplets of testicle blood upon what came to be known as Aphrodite's Rock, from which the Furies were born. Chronos had good reason, by the way—Uranus hated all his children and hid them away in a secret compartment inside his wife, Gaia. Gaia begged Chronos to cut off his father's testicles, so he did. But Uranus had a reason, too: he knew one of his children would kill him. The rock where all this happened is located in Paphos, Cyprus. Climbing it is prohibited.

It's too tidy: what makes us love is the sibling of what wants to kill us? I want the myths to spiral out toward formlessness, toward freedom, toward life . . . but since that isn't what they do, I correct them to my liking by forgetting some parts or refusing to learn them completely. In a pinch, when I remember too much or can't forget enough, I comfort myself in the different versions, many of them contradictory, and then I'm free.

I learn, for instance, that prior to Aeschylus, the story of how the Furies got renamed the Eumenides was different. It wasn't to appease them but out of fear: it was a way mortals could refer to them in secret. A code. "These Furies are crones, with snakes for hair, dogs' heads, coal-black bodies, bats' wings, and bloodshot eyes," says Robert Graves. "Their victims die in torment." You call them Eumenides, the kindly ones, so as not to arouse their attention.

It isn't true, as some accounts claim, that someone like Uranus "worried" or "feared" his children would kill him. *He knew it to be true.* He knew it the way you know it's cold out: by living. He just didn't know which one would do it. And a fact, once apprehended, can nauseate you from within, like a bug-bombed house. A fact can be worse than the horrible act it inspires.

*

You aren't supposed to swim out to the rock, which the high tide overtakes, and the sea is rough. Some believe if you swim around the rock three times—if you take on that risk—you'll find love. I'd do anything to keep MJ in love with me, is what I think, and circling a rock is the absolute least of it. "Don't leave me," I'd say to her, pulling on my trunks. So what if there's some chop out there? *Loving is not suffering* is what I think, and I am almost right. There are warning signs on the beach but they're all Greek to me. What is it, this test—

proving something, proof of something? The water so cold it deletes your brain? Stop thinking, Aphrodite says. Just swim. This is how she pulls me back into my body, which is the only place she can lay her gift. But I hate deleting my brain. I resist it. I start writing sentences in my head about MJ. I remember a paper bag of pastries. I remember many colors of nail and lip. I remember a thought that rose in me as if from a crane. The thought was: nothing else would do. "Her voice is syrup and it opiates me," I write in my head. *Swim*, Aphrodite says. *Swim, motherfucker.*

I learned about swimming around the rock on Trip Advisor. According to one review, the tuna salad at a café at the top of the hill might be worth it. But not everyone reports a positive experience. A user named SunnyLondoner claimed in February of 2016 that Aphrodite's Rock is "just a rock"; in June of 2015, Paddy T said it was "a rock—a pebble beach—unspectacular" and fantasized about digging a hole nearby and hanging a sign for "APHRODITE'S TOILET." Jhste from Glasgow said it was "Nowt to see," in the same summer (2015) that a user named KenHenBag called it "Aphrodite nonsense." TravelingGirl48's May 2014 review reads in full:

"What can i say its a rock in the sea. Thats it same as every other rock in the sea with its own myth. Forget it."

It seems like TravelingGirl48 is alluding to a preponderance of mythical sea rocks I don't know about, all of them superior to Aphrodite's. I picture these rocks poking their heads up through the sea like meerkats. I learn the name for such rocks—sea stacks—and her fantasy of an ocean full of sea stacks, which are themselves replete with meaning, seems to me the most basic human wish. I picture her as MJ in the bow cockpit of a small boat, a hat screwed down tight on her head. The wind and wake, lunch on her mind but first one more rock with its own myth to check out. I think of Ivan Ilyich close to death saying to himself, "What do I want? To live and not suffer." I don't want her to suffer. I want her to live and not to suffer the way Aphrodite's Rock made her suffer. I want her to find a rock that tells a story she can internalize and then shed, a crab who walks out of its home.

*

Joan Didion says she felt like a bag of spiders to us because her experiences are supposed to help us. When we finish a book we're supposed to know better?

It's not derivative if I swam in Portuguese Bend in real life. But I should not include in my book a passage about it, if I did. The winter after Noelle died I swam with MJ on Venice Beach, 32.0 miles from Portuguese Bend. All clear. Joan Didion says "you had to feel the swell change" to other grievers because it's a metaphor. It means there are delicacies around. If the cave can dry out, that means it can swell, too, and be swam in.

On Venice Beach MJ took off her boots and we fell in love. We have a picture. "I'm not using one of you with him," she said to a condom I took out.

BOYER

I don't know where I put my wedding ring but I remember I kept it in a white sunglasses case for years. I remember wanting to fly Noelle's ashes to the desert where we got married and I remember in one dream I bought the ashes their own ticket and buckled a seat belt around them. I remember the day I learned ashes have bone in them. I remember this because of something Noelle's sister asked me: *when you decide where to scatter the ashes please save some for us*, so five years after she died I bought a twelve pack of mason jars because they were not for sale individually. I bought a navy blue gift bag twice the size of a mason jar. Then I went next door to the supermarket and bought a dozen white roses. I put all these in my car and drove to my parents' house. I told my father I was ready for Noelle's ashes. He brought them out, and a funnel, and we poured them from the box into the mason jars, three in total. I asked him for rubber bands and I trimmed the roses to size and attached some to each mason jar and then I drove to Noelle's sister's house and Noelle's sister said, "oh, there's bone in there, okay." And I left and picked up Suzanne and drove us to Island Beach State Park where we all used to go. And Noelle would make us little sandwiches out of baguette and apples and brie while telling stories and she would swim so far out until we got scared and waved her in, but she would never come in. But then she would. Suzanne and I didn't say much. I didn't know who was in charge. We sat next to each other in the sand and we both had a mason jar. Bone in there, okay. Then I stood up and walked into the ocean and turned mine upside down and that was it. But then I saw Suzanne a little way up the coast and she was walking and sifting the ashes through one hand. Is Suzanne better at it than me, I wondered. And that was the last time I failed Noelle, by upending her all at once without ceremony on a gray afternoon, a week before I married MJ.

*

When we buy the house on Boyer, MJ gets to work scraping off the popcorn ceilings, spraying them with water and then drawing a huge blade across them again and again for weeks, the textured paint dropping to the tarps like dead bugs flicked off a roof.

Now we can see the hundred-year-old plaster beneath, cracked and gouged and multi-colored. I skim coat it with drywall mud. It takes so long I get muscles in my right arm and a rash on my side I can't explain. The mud dries into the synthetic white of nightmares, and sanding it turns the room into a cloud of toxic dust. It covers me in a suit as I move through it. I play the same songs over and over, a lullaby for the ceilings. Outside on the porch with a beer, the neighbors joke I'm a ghost. The music plays on inside. "A ghost of what," I ask, but they don't hear me.

It rains and we remember the rain. We prefer the meadow to the woods and where we live now to where we lived before. We walk slowly on the walk home and we wish to walk slower.

We didn't expect to stay in love in the first place.

*

The house on Boyer is on the brink of the woods at the edge of the city. The only way to get there is on Lincoln Drive, which hairpins through the trees and along a creek and causes a good many serious accidents. Many years ago, the brakes of Teddy Pendergrass's Rolls Royce Silver Spirit gave out on this road, and the car jumped the median and crashed into the trees. We like to drive so fast on this road that danger can't put its finger on us. We drive it in silence, make the car into a slider that zips the road shut. Time and speed eat our fear: the outer rind at first, and then the soft middle, bite by bite.

*

In the mornings, waiting for the coffee to steep, I tidy the kitchen of its signs of the previous day's life, returning everything to its first position. I feel a righteous pride as I impale the paper towel roll back onto its spindle. Like the Zen master who, afraid he would habituate to the ongoingness of life, had his assistant periodically rearrange his kitchen, rendering even the simplest culinary task difficult, one day MJ removes the dishwasher silverware basket and dumps it into the utensil drawer, where it forms a pile. She turns to face me, a wildness at the edges of her mouth.

The crickets become such an issue in the basement, so jumpy, their antennae so whiskery and long, I resort to the glue traps. On which they wiggle to death, I guess. One is so big I think he looks at me, surprised.

We put my tent in the very fast car and head out west. A honeymoon. Someone mentioned you could have stark thoughts out there, ones you couldn't produce at home. Starkness, I remember someone else telling me, is when the tape measure sucks back into itself. It would feel good to be in love somewhere stark, we think. Maybe see some animals. It's closer than you think. Two days, three tops.

We guard ourselves against the silly epiphanies our brains keep trying to produce. An epiphany purports to be stark but it lies; only a stark thought can tell you what you actually are. We want what no therapist or friend can offer, only a mountain or a length of river or a garish sunset. We want to know who we are.

We notice how the sun falls on the other at different times, inside the car and out, how lovely, how possible it would be to stretch the legs of the feeling it gives us. We find each other very funny, very beautiful, very actual. Breath in the tent, beer in the cupholder, breath in the tent, according to the sun's path. Is this what it is, we wonder. The map says we're thirty-six hours from home.

I learn axles aren't called that anymore—they're called constant velocity joints, and we break one driving up a mountain. We try, failing, to describe the effect the wilderness is having on us. I remember the aggressive specificity of the stars, the moon so late to rise and so bright it wakes us up to clip the fly back on. When the sun comes up, we walk the empty meadows, guessing badly at the names of trees and flowers. We drink tequila slowly over gas station ice, which produces the entire Milky Way all at once, so low and clear in the sky it has the effect of a joke.

We bring the car down the mountain with what feels like care, and then drive hard through the smoke blowing in from Oregon, south down I-15. It's like driving through a ream of paper. We fill up the tank, and smoke, and fill it again. We squeegee the windshield and swipe our card for ice. On turns, the very fast car clicks a tongue I didn't know it had: that's the axle. It's 115 degrees before noon. We sneak into a hotel pool and float alongside a credit card executive from New Jersey.

We see both Boulders but prefer the Boulder in Utah, where we listen to Tanya Tucker and smoke cigarettes and pull over as often as we want. We take a road going sixty-seven miles toward Lake Powell in Arizona, the paved road giving way to dirt and the dirt to red rock dust, the landscape orgasmically Martian to the extent that you alternate between the platitudes of the gob-smacked and getting horny in a way that doesn't feel remotely earthbound and won't be satisfied, ever.

*

Back on Boyer: "Better to know the devil you know," she says. She paints half the bathroom and we leave it that way. She pictures a net inside us through which the high tide of tragedy comes and goes. I picture it too. We walk home, wishing for home, taking the long way, extra time for the wish. I look into, but cannot afford, sponsoring a goat for her birthday.

When she tells our friends her recurring sex dream—"and I have this huge dick and I fuck these women…"—they ask me what it's like to love her.

"It should listen to jazz because that's a crazy thing humans invented," she says about our hypothetical baby. We're always walking home on the walk home.

"You're not putting that in the basement," she says to me about every object I want to put down there. Whatever we'll ever own she wants to see, and she doesn't want to own much.

*

Our friends get married where Noelle's funeral was, at a state park in my hometown. We drink and eat and dance. When I'm transported by memories of the funeral, my thoughts about that sadness are banal. I send my sister a text of gratitude that embarrasses me, and when she responds, I can't bear to read it.

It's night but not late. Dark but early. I remember learning the word nostalgia means something or other about being nauseous for home. You lay one piece of paper on top of another, on top of another, and what's on each piece matters but also doesn't. I remember Josh tying my tie for me. I remember taking a pill in the porta potty. I remember my sister struggled to compose herself while reading a poem and I stood up and held on to her, a poem on four legs, trying, and we stood, reading, where the bass player in the wedding band is gyrating to Stevie Wonder.

The band's excellence grates on me. I walk out of the pavilion, away from the twinkling string lights, to the parking lot. The crunch of its gravel is so old to me I could be a boy, or dead, or it could be tomorrow, hungover, scooped-out and penitent.

*

MJ attaches a sentence from Lydia Davis to the wall by the door on Boyer: "The house does not seem big enough to hold all the people who keep appearing in it at different times." She fixes it to the wall by driving a small nail through the page.

Welcome, we say. Mattress on the living room floor, sheets on the couch. There is no Lydia Davis sentence about the relatively small number of objects that pass through a single human life. You're going to have to reuse them. You're going to have to wash the sheets and let someone else sleep on them. *Does it overwhelm you* asks the monk and I say all the time and he says *Is that why you come down here when people come over* and I say I don't come down here every time and he says *Is that why you sometimes come down here when people come over* and I say yes. I switch the laundry. Sometimes I keep switching it, dryer back to washer.

But over here by the basement window. Where the smartest crickets congregate, the ones who avoided the glue traps like jewel thieves. Where this narrow slice of light pushes itself through the window is where—look with me—

—*Are they looking*, asks the monk—

—I think so, I say—

Look where it lands, look where the light pushes through.

Look where it lands. It lands on the tent.

I have a dream about MJ and me and the very fast car. We drive the car so fast and so hard it comes apart—first the doors pull themselves off and get sucked away, then the windshield explodes and we feel the hot air, then the rest of the car's body separates from the chassis and the back seats shoot straight up into the sky but we keep driving. Both of us are howling. Soon the tires burn away and it's just us in our seats on the chassis, which is heating up, the heat is everywhere, sparks are raining upward as the chassis grinds into the highway. We understand what we've wanted all along was to extend the inner nature of the very fast car to its absurd end. And we've figured out something else. We had to drive the very fast car to this point to learn it—the knowledge was not available at normal speeds. Now everything is hot, too hot to misunderstand: this is the fire we can stay inside. It's ours because we say so. We didn't build it. We claim it.

Upstairs, MJ is playing jazz, something easy on the ears. Down here it's a heartbeat coming through the joists. A joist, like a bone, will squeak if you dance on it.

*

It's MJ's copy of *The Death of Ivan Ilyich* I've been reading, in the big maroon hardcover Everyman's Library edition. So it's she who did the underlining on page 163 in thin pencil:

> "Maybe I did not live as I ought to have done," it suddenly occurred to him. "But how could that be, when I did everything properly?" he replied, and immediately dismissed from his mind this, the sole solution of all the riddles of life and death, as something quite impossible.

What's worse, that Ivan nearly solves the mystery of existence only to dismiss it? Or that he dismisses it *immediately*? Was it Tolstoy, desperate to become useful late in his life, who learned how to cobble shoes? Who was she when she held that pencil and made these marks, like the toes a ghost leaves behind? Who was she when she wanted to remember all this? Her old self is a ghost I can't meet. I remember pulling up in daylight even though I didn't. Today we pull up to the meadow at dusk. We meet this guy who says it's a hawk, not a vulture. "But what's the harm if I call it a vulture," I ask him. It's far and long gone by, could be anything—should be anything. Dusk light soaks the tall porcelain grass literally forever. MJ falls behind to gather some into a bouquet: "here, a meadow," she says, but I can't see her, not even a little, it's too bright, too bright in this place that no one can force us to leave or rename.

Are you sure they're good for hiking?

She pulls her boots on, on, on.

I've said my little sentence about how Noelle did it but it's not enough. I'm supposed to repeat it or sing it, I'm supposed to make it prettier and prettier until it's too pretty and then you'll call me a monster. *You*, it's *you*. You expect me to pile other sentences around it until a theory appears—something you can know. And by knowing, ignore: because knowing is what happens after. But I don't want after. I want here.

So I didn't want to write this book after all, it seems. I didn't want to but I did. Noelle didn't want to live but for thirty-nine years she did. Then she wanted to die and she did that, too. *How many more do they want*, asks the monk. I was deranged after she decided to die and then years passed and then I wasn't. It was like when the sun rises in a school play.

*

—I couldn't bear to hear Neil Young anymore and I didn't think I would ever—

—but eventually I took MJ to see him—

—and we took off our shoes in the park beforehand and drank a rosé my wine expert friend gave us—

—something she bought in Brooklyn, not far from where I was when Noelle was killed by herself—

—not far from Brooklyn Bridge Park, where I sat with my friends and surely some of what we drank that night was rosé, there was so much wine, it was a celebration and—

—something I always forget to say—

—my friends played a trick—

—they memorized a poem of mine and the six of them recited it to me—

—like me, they could not have known what Noelle was doing—

—what she was doing then—

—and like them, I attached no special meaning to the final line of that poem—

—"it takes forever"—

—I didn't walk all the way to Harlem after the celebration, could not have, but that's how I remember it—

—I remember the Columbia building, the one from *Ghostbusters*—

—I took a woozy picture of it doused in what I thought was moonlight but it wasn't—

—it was ordinary streetlight and I couldn't have walked all that way, I would not have—

—Alex lived at 98 Morningside Ave—

—I bet he showed off and got us a cab—

—which would place me in the cab when Noelle died—

—it took so long for me to get home to her—

—I called so many times, I knew—

—I called Suzanne I know I'm being paranoid I said—

—Noelle was already dead on the floor when I said that—

—on the tile—

—I see myself waking up in Harlem—

—then on the subway, then on the bus on the turnpike, all the while calling and calling—

—please I said—

—please I'm scared—

—and I was—

—I was so scared—

—a scared boy who slept—

—in his clothes and rode—

—home in those clothes—

—I only wanted my wife to be alive—

—but there was no one—

—no one to give me that gift—

*

I don't want to know if loving MJ was part of my grief or if Noelle dying was part of loving MJ. I don't want to say it depends on where you begin the story. I don't want to be the person who says that.

I wonder if everyone wants to be something other than what they mainly are. Is there even one story that doesn't involve somebody pretending or wishing to be someone else?

Here's my story: every morning a sad man tiptoes out of his past. But he can only get so far in a day.

My story is about the beginning of life with MJ, when I didn't totally know who she was. It's about the next part, too, when I did. And the next part, when I fell in love with her (a) from the beginning or (b) on Venice Beach several months after we met or (c) before Venice Beach, when she showed me she knew who she was, or (d) on the way to the CVS or (e) a time and place I've not yet remembered. It's about the next part, when I hated myself for loving her but didn't know. And the next, when I realized I hated myself. And the next, when I wrote a whole book to figure it out and the book takes forever and sometimes MJ says "you have that blue-gray look" and I lie and say I'm just tired from work and she says "you have that demented haggard face thing going on" or "the sadness pouring off you is contagious" and she goes to New Hampshire to be with her mother and returns in a new flannel shirt. And my story is about how I fell in love with her (f) then, for how she knew to get out and how to return.

It's about how she'll cook every night for weeks and then

one day stop: "I'm not doing that anymore," she'll say, going upstairs with her books. It's about this nature of hers. And the word for it is boring: it's honesty. It's about her closing her eyes for a beat and it's about how she opens them and tells the truth on the exhale. It's called *The Hose of Truth*. The end of it goes like this:

Would you like to finish your story, once and for all?

I was the rat and I was desperate for MJ to know I had once been human, a charmer who knew things rather than a disgusting outcast. I even resented her for sheltering me in her house and in her heart. You aren't supposed to do that. Noelle, I thought, would have killed the rat on sight and would have been correct for it. Noelle would have killed the rat and then led me, the human, to the couch, where she would lie on her side and I would lie on her hip, both of us looking in the same direction, at the TV, and we would watch a movie, snug there, our two bodies a perfect fit. We wouldn't have even mentioned the rat. Why would you mention the rat?

So how did you become human again?

MJ and I don't fit as well on the couch as Noelle and I did because MJ is much taller than Noelle was, nearly as tall as I am. We can't curl up on it like pups of the same litter. Whenever we try, it's never long before one of us feels cramped. It took time for us to invent a system: her over there and me over here, and first I rub her feet and then she flips around, puts her head on my lap and every so often her hand on my thigh absentmindedly in that way that makes you feel like a prince. This is how we watched *The Departed*—by the way it was me, it turns out, who woke up scared when Martin Sheen was thrown from the roof. Not her. I had fallen asleep sitting up, my feet on the coffee table and her head on my lap, and when I jumped awake I ejected her head from my lap and she yelped.

What's your point?

MJ is tall. She likes to wear her great-grandmother's big red coat in the winter, and I have been told I have a funny walk. So wherever we go, we are easily seen.

But what's your point?

On what I didn't know at the time was the last day of my life as the rat, I took MJ to dinner in the old neighborhood, not far from the so-blue house and not far from her old apartment on Collins. The neighborhood had changed so much, but we were just happy to be in love, me with her and she, I guess, with the rat. It was a warm day, one of the first warm days of early spring. MJ was wearing her big red coat. The sidewalks were teeming with people and the streets were gridlocked with cars. We had to park far from the restaurant, and as we walked, something awful happened.

Is this the ending, finally?

Some guys in an SUV drove up alongside us at the same speed as we were walking. It was a narrow street. It was intimate. They were shrieking something I'll never forget and smirking like real bullies, professional at it. They would ogle MJ and then stare me down and shriek the same thing over and over, the wheels of the SUV just barely rolling. It was like they knew everything—like they could tell just by looking at us that something was off, like they knew I was too disgusting for MJ, undeserving of this beauty in her big red coat.

Why?

I worried everyone thought it and only managed to suppress it out of love or tact. Or maybe pity. As if to say: this sad rat has bigger fish to fry. Let us not punish him additionally with the truth but rather shelter him from it by making our eyes kind. But these guys in the SUV, they gave me the gift of their rancor. It was in their eyes, which they made as wide as they could as if to take in more of what disgusted them, and it rang out sarcastically when they shrieked.

What did they shriek?

"Lucky man!" And then they turned to me smirking, and repeated it louder: "Lucky lucky man!" We were stuck with them unless we turned around and walked the other way, which we were too proud to do.

Why did they call you lucky?

I felt my body warming up. I was so mad and so scared.

Did you know them?

I looked into the eyes of the driver. I could tell he'd been looking for me. The eyes of the others said the same. They'd been searching. They'd been calibrating my punishment. I don't know, maybe MJ's big red coat is how they found me.

"These," I said not calmly to MJ, "are the Furies."

The Furies in an SUV near the so-blue house?

They had come to remind me of my broken oath and then kill me. I was the rat who thought he could take this woman in a big red coat out to dinner near the so-blue house like it was all no big deal. Like Noelle never existed. Like Noelle was just a preamble to this new part of my life. Like I hadn't gotten rid of everything that reminded me of her and moved on. They were here to kill me for this.

What happened next?

The SUV stopped at the light and all three turned to face me squarely. The driver had his right hand rakishly at twelve o'clock on the wheel and his left arm out the window. I could almost touch it, that's how narrow the street was.

Did they keep shrieking it?

Again and again. Over and over, louder and louder. People were looking. There was concern. But I knew the Furies were only doing their job. I knew they had to kill me.

What did you say?

First I tried some sentences that did not work. I prayed that if I confessed enough true things to the Furies they would spare me and then I would be clean and could love cleanly, without having to push my love through so much shame. I was brainstorming confessions. I knew some of them would be about the couch because other than the fact that MJ and I don't fit very well on it, there's something else important about it: sometimes it felt like Noelle was on the couch with me rather than MJ. It wasn't that I saw Noelle. It was a type of confusion, like the wires of the past and present had been crossed. I tried to think of a good example to confess. One night MJ put on *The Getaway* and I started rubbing her feet. I only learned recently it's the pads under her toes she really likes me to rub—so close to the undersides of her toes, like my fingers are saying something very indirect to them. She said something about Steve McQueen—he'd just rope-swung into a lake after getting out of prison—and when I looked over . . . it's not that she *was* Noelle. That's not what it was. It was like a memory of Noelle was interfering—like God was tuning it in using his huge dial. But it wasn't just one memory, it was all of them. It was like what they call a group of mortgages prepared as an instrument for rich people to play around with: a pool. So this pool of memories was being dialed in by God, thirteen years' worth of movies and eating and curling up like pups of the same litter, and sadness and happiness, and fighting and making up. I hated this pool so much. What was I supposed to do with it? And I hated myself for hating it. I should have been alone in my tent with my grief rather than there, fishing for blowjobs and being in love and confusing the present for the past.

What was MJ doing?

She was looking at the Furies with interest and pity, like they were a carload of child prodigies. I could tell she wasn't afraid of them at all—she reached into a pocket of her big red coat for something and then stepped into the street, stood in front of the SUV, craned her neck out toward the windshield, pursed her lips and used it as a mirror to freshen up her lipstick.

Did you join her in the street?

Just then, the back window came down, the one on the driver's side closest to me, like a curtain at the opening of a play but in reverse, and the backseat Fury shrieked his lines. He was the worst of them. His face looked like meat and there was blood spraying from his mouth, droplets of it falling into the opening the window disappeared into.

I had fought hard to avoid learning that love is merely a container we climb into. I was done fighting. MJ turned to face me. "There's something you need to do," she said, and then she did something very strange. She grabbed the lapels of her big red coat, one in each hand, and with a shrug popped the coat up and then below the line of her shoulders. Then she straightened out both arms, snapping her elbows, and with a subtle wiggling of her wrists, the big red coat began to slide down her arms. From where I stood on the sidewalk, the coat—heavy and wool, hers since the beginning of time—looked weightless. She pulled her left hand out first and held it aloft for a moment as the coat completed its slide down her right arm. For an instant it seemed the coat might touch the ground but she managed to work her right hand into the right shoulder just in time, and then she brought her left hand down and gently, so gently, worked it into the left shoulder. When she reached this final position, standing in the road square in front of the SUV, she cracked it once like a whip, holding the big red coat aloft as though to show the

Furies its red silk lining. It's really a beautiful coat. I think it was rippling, the very bottom of it, an inch or two off the street, in the spring breeze.

The backseat fury had his entire meaty doghead and half his upper body out the window to ogle her, shrieking his lines over and over, leaving no space between the end of one and the beginning of the next.

"This is what I do for him," MJ shouted to the backseat Fury. "Just like this, whenever he wants." The breeze nipped at the hair around her ears. She turned to me. "Lucky, lucky man," she said, and extended her arm to invite me.

I took a step down into the street toward the car. Everyone was watching. It felt like I was on TV. All three Furies had their dogheads out of their windows now, and they were shrieking and shrieking and the SUV was stippled in their blood, and so was the street, and everyone was watching, and MJ was doing capework, her shins nearly making contact with the SUV's grill, the big red coat her only protection from it. Her face was turned to mine and she kept saying it, quietly, "lucky lucky man," over and over, slowly and calmly, and smiling so big I could see her gums, so big I could see into the darkness of her mouth.

Then the light turned green and the SUV started rolling forward ever so slowly. MJ kept waving the big red coat in front of it, daring it, daring the Furies.

"Tell them," she said.

I took a single step off the sidewalk into the street and toward the driver. The wheel was covered in blood, thick smears of it, and the dashboard too, and he was shrieking his lines so hard his body was squirming a little, and in the squirming I could hear the rubbery sound of his body sliding around on the blood.

What did you say?

It felt like I'd already confessed everything else, like I'd exhausted my confessions, worked through nearly all of them and now only one remained. I didn't even feel particularly clear-headed, but I reached my hand into the muck in my head and produced a final confession. It had been waiting for me this whole time. It was slippery from the muck, but I squeezed it hard.

I thought of the couple who bought the so-blue house. I thought of them on their couch and I wondered if they were really in love and I hoped they were. I knew from driving past, which I did often, that they'd kept our curtains—white ones Noelle hemmed to fit the windows. I loved those curtains. They felt grown-up and respectable to me, and I remembered the night we hung them I ironed them one by one, and the so-blue house felt like a workshop and I would have gone on, ironing and ironing for all time, but soon I had finished—the so-blue house only had four windows in front and two in back—so we hung them on cheap tension rods and that's where they stayed, blacking out the light.

What did you say?

I reached my hand out toward the window, and he took it in his. I squeezed it with affection and shook it. "You're kind for saying that," I said, meaning it. "I'm a lucky man." I did feel lucky. Then his hand lost all its grip. It was the limp hand of a teenager. His friends in the SUV looked like students who missed a deadline but weren't going to lie about it. They looked like good kids. MJ brought together the two shoulders of her big red coat and draped it over her left forearm, stepping away from the SUV, which rolled on through the intersection.

And do you think that's true?

My confession felt final when I said it, but as soon as it came out of my mouth I felt how many more there would be, various and bright as holes in the sky. It was true: I was lucky. I could see it. The narrow street was cast in shadow and we were still standing in it, traffic gliding past our toes. I took the hand of the woman I love and she gestured down the block with her eyes toward the restaurant, its brick façade blanched white by the sun. We stayed there so long. We ate all the pasta we possibly could.

Acknowledgments

Thank you to my friends who read and improved this book: Cory Brown, Fady Joudah, Joe Kenyon, Zach Savich, Taije Silverman, and Sidney Wade. To Hilary Plum, Caryl Pagel, and Zach Peckham at the Poetry Center: thank you. Thank you to all my friends who went with me through the days this book describes, some of you named but many not. Thank you to my family. And thank you to MJ, who took this book upstairs and made it what it is.

Thanks to the following works, which are quoted in the text:

The Oresteia of Aeschylus, translated by Ted Hughes (FSG, 2000).

Collected Shorter Fiction: Volume 1, Leo Tolstoy, translated by Aylmer and Louise Maude (Everyman's Library, 2001).

Dollhouse, Elaine Terranova (Off the Grid Press, 2013).

The Greek Myths, Robert Graves (Penguin Classics, 2012).

"I have walked through the world's great kitchen" is from Wallace Stegner, *The Spectator Bird*.

Now You Can Join the Others, Taije Silverman (LSU Press, 2022).

Michael Loughran's work has appeared in *Boston Review*, *Indiana Review*, *Harvard Review*, *Tin House*, and elsewhere. He lives in Philadelphia and teaches at the Community College of Philadelphia. *Windower* is his first book.

RECENT CLEVELAND STATE UNIVERSITY POETRY CENTER PUBLICATIONS

edited by Caryl Pagel & Hilary Plum

POETRY

Mechanical Bull by Rennie Ament

World'd Too Much: The Selected Poetry of Russell Atkins
ed. Kevin Prufer and Robert E. McDonough

Advantages of Being Evergreen by Oliver Baez Bendorf

The Devil's Workshop by Xavier Cavazos

Ordinary Entanglement by Melissa Dickey

Dream Boat by Shelley Feller

My Fault by Leora Fridman

Orient by Nicholas Gulig

Twice There Was A Country by Alen Hamza

Age of Glass by Anna Maria Hong

outside voices, please by Valerie Hsiung

In One Form to Find Another by Jane Lewty

50 Water Dreams by Siwar Masannat

Mule: 10th Anniversary Edition by Shane McCrae

daughterrarium by Sheila McMullin

The Bees Make Money in the Lion by Lo Kwa Mei-en

Residuum by Martin Rock

Festival by Broc Rossell

Sun Cycle by Anne Lesley Selcer

Arena by Lauren Shapiro

Bottle the Bottles the Bottles the Bottles by Lee Upton

Innocence by Michael Joseph Walsh

No Doubt I Will Return A Different Man by Tobias Wray

ESSAYS

I want to start by saying by Samuel Ace

I Liked You Better Before I Knew You So Well
by James Allen Hall

A Bestiary by Lily Hoang

Codependence by Amy Long

Telephone: Essays in Two Voices
by Brenda Miller and Julie Marie Wade

The Leftovers by Shaelyn Smith

TRANSLATIONS

No One Knows Their Blood Type by Maya Abu Al-Hayyat,
translated by Hazem Jamjoum

Almost Obscene by Raúl Gómez Jattin,
translated by Katherine M. Hedeen and Olivia Lott

Scorpionic Sun by Mohammed Khaïr-Eddine,
translated by Conor Bracken

I Burned at the Feast: Selected Poems of Arseny Tarkovsky,
translated by Philip Metres and Dimitri Psurtsev

for a complete list of titles visit CSUPoetryCenter.com